D1207497

Free Trade

Other Books of Related Interest:

Opposing Viewpoints Series
America's Global Influence

Human Rights

Labor Unions

At Issue Series
What Is the Future of the U.S. Economy?

Corporate Corruption

Does Outsourcing Harm America?

Contemporary Issues Companion Series
Consumerism

Current Controversies Series
Developing Nations

Globalization

"Congress shall make
no law . . . abridging
the freedom of speech,
or of the press."

First Amendment to the U.S. Constitution

The basic foundation of our democracy is the First Amendment guarantee of freedom of expression. The Opposing Viewpoints Series is dedicated to the concept of this basic freedom and the idea that it is more important to practice it than to enshrine it.

Free Trade

Mitchell Young, Book Editor

GREENHAVEN PRESS
A part of Gale, Cengage Learning

Detroit • New York • San Francisco • New Haven, Conn • Waterville, Maine • London

Christine Nasso, *Publisher*
Elizabeth Des Chenes, *Managing Editor*

© 2009 Greenhaven Press, a part of Gale, Cengage Learning.

Gale and Greenhaven Press are registered trademarks used herein under license.

For more information, contact:
Greenhaven Press
27500 Drake Rd.
Farmington Hills, MI 48331-3535
Or you can visit our Internet site at gale.cengage.com

For product information and technology assistance, contact us at

Gale Customer Support, 1-800-877-4253
For permission to use material from this text or product, submit all requests online at www.cengage.com/permissions

Further permissions questions can be emailed to permissionrequest@cengage.com

Articles in Greenhaven Press anthologies are often edited for length to meet page requirements. In addition, original titles of these works are changed to clearly present the main thesis and to explicitly indicate the author's opinion. Every effort is made to ensure that Greenhaven Press accurately reflects the original intent of the authors. Every effort has been made to trace the owners of copyrighted material.

Cover photograph reproduced by permission of Andrew Rich/Photodisc/Getty Images.

LIBRARY OF CONGRESS CATALOGING-IN-PUBLICATION DATA

Free trade / Mitchell Young, book editor.
   p. cm. -- (Opposing viewpoints)
   Includes bibliographical references and index.
   ISBN-13: 978-0-7377-4000-4 (hardcover)
   ISBN-13: 978-0-7377-4001-1 (pbk.)
   1. Free trade--Juvenile literature. 2. Free trade--United States--Juvenile literature. 3. Free trade--Environmental aspects--Juvenile literature. 4. Commercial policy--Juvenile literature. I. Young, Mitchell.
   HF1713.F7353 2009
   382'.71--dc22
                                  2008026060

Printed in the United States of Americ
1 2 3 4 5 6 7 12 11 10 09 08

382.71 FRE 2009

Free trade.

Contents

Chapter 3: How Does Free Trade Affect Labor and the Environment?

Chapter 4: What Trade Policies and Practices Are Most Beneficial?

Why Consider
Opposing Viewpoints?

"The only way in which a human being can make some approach to knowing the whole of a subject is by hearing what can be said about it by persons of every variety of opinion and studying all modes in which it can be looked at by every character of mind. No wise man ever acquired his wisdom in any mode but this."

John Stuart Mill

In our media-intensive culture it is not difficult to find differing opinions. Thousands of newspapers and magazines and dozens of radio and television talk shows resound with differing points of view. The difficulty lies in deciding which opinion to agree with and which "experts" seem the most credible. The more inundated we become with differing opinions and claims, the more essential it is to hone critical reading and thinking skills to evaluate these ideas. Opposing Viewpoints books address this problem directly by presenting stimulating debates that can be used to enhance and teach these skills. The varied opinions contained in each book examine many different aspects of a single issue. While examining these conveniently edited opposing views, readers can develop critical thinking skills such as the ability to compare and contrast authors' credibility, facts, argumentation styles, use of persuasive techniques, and other stylistic tools. In short, the Opposing Viewpoints Series is an ideal way to attain the higher-level thinking and reading skills so essential in a culture of diverse and contradictory opinions.

In addition to providing a tool for critical thinking, Opposing Viewpoints books challenge readers to question their own strongly held opinions and assumptions. Most people form their opinions on the basis of upbringing, peer pressure, and personal, cultural, or professional bias. By reading carefully balanced opposing views, readers must directly confront new ideas as well as the opinions of those with whom they disagree. This is not to simplistically argue that everyone who reads opposing views will—or should—change his or her opinion. Instead, the series enhances readers' understanding of their own views by encouraging confrontation with opposing ideas. Careful examination of others' views can lead to the readers' understanding of the logical inconsistencies in their own opinions, perspective on why they hold an opinion, and the consideration of the possibility that their opinion requires further evaluation.

Evaluating Other Opinions

To ensure that this type of examination occurs, Opposing Viewpoints books present all types of opinions. Prominent spokespeople on different sides of each issue as well as well-known professionals from many disciplines challenge the reader. An additional goal of the series is to provide a forum for other, less known, or even unpopular viewpoints. The opinion of an ordinary person who has had to make the decision to cut off life support from a terminally ill relative, for example, may be just as valuable and provide just as much insight as a medical ethicist's professional opinion. The editors have two additional purposes in including these less known views. One, the editors encourage readers to respect others' opinions—even when not enhanced by professional credibility. It is only by reading or listening to and objectively evaluating others' ideas that one can determine whether they are worthy of consideration. Two, the inclusion of such viewpoints encourages the important critical thinking skill of objectively evaluating an author's credentials and bias. This evaluation will illuminate an author's reasons for taking a particular stance on an issue and will aid in readers' evaluation of the author's ideas.

It is our hope that these books will give readers a deeper understanding of the issues debated and an appreciation of the complexity of even seemingly simple issues when good and honest people disagree. This awareness is particularly important in a democratic society such as ours in which people enter into public debate to determine the common good. Those with whom one disagrees should not be regarded as enemies but rather as people whose views deserve careful examination and may shed light on one's own.

Thomas Jefferson once said that "difference of opinion leads to inquiry, and inquiry to truth." Jefferson, a broadly educated man, argued that "if a nation expects to be ignorant and free . . . it expects what never was and never will be." As individuals and as a nation, it is imperative that we consider the opinions of others and examine them with skill and discernment. The Opposing Viewpoints Series is intended to help readers achieve this goal.

David L. Bender and Bruno Leone,
Founders

Introduction

> "When producers create goods they are comparatively skilled at, such as Germans producing beer and the French producing wine, those goods increase in abundance and quality." Marian L. Tupy, Washington Times, *January 3, 2006.*

> "The rise of free trade has eroded America's industrial base and with it our sovereignty." Patrick J. Buchanan, American Conservative, *August 11, 2003.*

Economists are divided on many issues, but nearly all agree that free trade is a good thing. This view is so influential that most U.S. politicians, both Democrat and Republican, liberal and conservative, claim to support free trade. However, with the growth of the Internet, worldwide investment, and large American trade deficits, a few economists and politicians are rethinking the traditional consensus on free trade.

The benefits of free trade have been touted for a long time, at least as far back as Adam Smith's *Wealth of Nations*, published in 1776. In some cases there is no denying the advantages of trade. For example, while Iceland could produce its own wine if it invested in greenhouses to grow grapes, it is better off putting money and labor into developing its fishing industry to take advantage of the rich waters that surround it. Icelanders could then trade fish to a country with a climate more naturally suited to wine production, such as Italy. This is a case of absolute advantage; each country has a natural ability to produce a specific good more efficiently than its trading partner.

Two countries may still benefit from trade even if one trading partner is more efficient at producing everything. The key here is what economists call opportunity costs—costs measured in terms of other goods rather than in dollars. A country can produce a limited amount of goods with its supply of labor. If it devotes one hundred hours of labor to producing wheat, that labor is not available for producing steel. If, say, it can produce either eight hundred bushels of wheat or four hundred tons of steel with that one hundred hours of labor, the opportunity cost of each ton of steel is two bushels of wheat (eight hundred bushels of wheat/four hundred tons of steel); conversely, each bushel of wheat "costs" one half of a ton of steel (four hundred tons of steel/eight hundred bushels of wheat).

Free-trade theory says that nations benefit from producing those goods for which they have the lowest opportunity costs. Let's say Country A can produce four hundred tons of steel or eight hundred bushels of wheat with its available labor, and Country B can produce two hundred tons of steel or two hundred bushels of wheat with its labor. Country A has an absolute advantage; with its labor supply, it can produce more steel and more wheat than Country B. However, Country A's opportunity cost of producing one ton of steel is two bushels of wheat, while Country B's cost of producing one ton of steel is one bushel of wheat. Country B is then said to have a comparative advantage in producing steel because its opportunity cost for producing steel, as measured by bushels of wheat, is lower than Country A's.

Theoretically both Country A and Country B will be better off if they specialize in producing the good in which they have a comparative advantage—in other words, the good for which they have the lowest opportunity cost—and then trade with the other country to meet their needs for other goods. To illustrate this, say each country in the above example devotes half its labor to producing steel, and half to wheat production in order to meet demand for wheat and steel. Country A will then produce two hundred tons of steel and four hundred bushels of wheat; Country B will produce one hundred tons of steel and one hundred bushels of wheat. Total production of the two countries is three hundred tons of steel and five hundred bushels of wheat. Now imagine that Country B specializes in steel production, where it has a comparative advantage. It produces two hundred tons of steel and no wheat. Country A produces the entire five hundred tons of wheat demanded by consumers of both countries. However, because of its comparative advantage in producing wheat, Country A can produce this amount with five-eighths of its available labor. The remaining three-eighths of its labor can be used to produce steel in the amount of three-eighths of four hundred tons, or 150 tons of steel. With this arrangement, total production of the two countries is five hundred tons of wheat, all of which is produced by Country A, and 350 tons of steel, two hundred tons produced by Country B, and 150 tons produced by Country A. Both nations are now better off because they have the same amount of wheat, but there are fifty more tons of steel available than if each has simply devoted half of its labor to wheat and half to steel.

The above example is a simplification of what happens in real life. One key complication is that even though more goods are available when countries specialize in their area of comparative advantage, the theory does not explain how any surplus (the extra fifty tons of steel in the example) is divided between the countries. However, even though the story is simplified, most economists believe that trade theory is a good approximation of actual events. Economists often cite the 1846 repeal of the Corn Laws, which restricted grain imports into Great Britain. Abolishing them allowed the country to import most of its food and employ most of its labor in manufacturing, initiating nearly a century of British economic dominance.

Recently, however, some economists have begun to rethink comparative advantage and the benefits of free trade. Revisionists such as Ralph Gomory and William Baumol point to the ease of investing in foreign countries today and the advantages of large-scale, concentrated industry to show that under certain conditions, trade can make workers in relatively wealthy countries worse off. Other writers disagree with the conventional view that free trade helped Britain after the repeal of the Corn Laws; Patrick J. Buchanan points out that both Germany and the United States grew faster than Britain in the nineteenth century, and both of the former had protectionist policies that guarded their industries from imports.

Doubts about free trade are also being felt in developing countries, which are increasingly competing with one another for market share. Dan Griswold, an expert at the pro-free-trade Cato Institute, notes that "producers in China are clearly cutting into Mexico's market share in several important manufacturing sectors" and are hurting Mexico's exports to the United States. In India, another country that is thought by many to have benefitted from trade, poor farmers are being squeezed by large multinational corporations that, since trade liberalization, have come to control the market for seed and fertilizer, according to activist Vandana Shiva.

Many facets of the controversy over free trade are examined in *Opposing Viewpoints: Free Trade*. Chapters present viewpoints on the following questions: Does Free Trade Help the American Economy? Does Free Trade Help the Developing World? How Does Free Trade Affect Labor and the Environment? What Trade Policies and Practices Are Most Beneficial? With ever-easier communications and transportation between nations, these issues will only grow in importance in the coming decades—and so will the debate about them.

OPPOSING
VIEWPOINTS®
SERIES

CHAPTER 1

Does Free Trade Help the American Economy?

Chapter Preface

Many Americans think of international trade only when it is associated with bad news such as plant closings, worker layoffs, or reports of ever-increasing trade deficits. It is little wonder then that free trade is unpopular with many segments of the public. This contrasts sharply with the opinions of American policy elites: Political and business leaders typically view free trade as a good thing. They have the support of economists, who are nearly unanimous in believing that trade benefits society despite the obvious dislocation of some workers and businesses by foreign competition.

Free traders point out that millions of American jobs rely on trade. Most obvious examples are workers in export-oriented industries, such as agriculture and aerospace. The entertainment industry also earns vast amounts of foreign revenue and employs tens of thousands of workers; some of those jobs would disappear if other countries did not have the dollars, earned through trade, to buy American films, music, and video games. Moreover, trade itself employs thousands of Americans—from longshoremen who handle imported goods in our ports to truckers who transport goods throughout the country to retail workers who sell imported goods. Supporters of free trade note that a factory that is forced to close due to foreign competition often makes the news, but the jobs created by free trade seldom get noticed. Finally, free traders claim that foreign goods are often cheaper and of higher quality than American-made products, thus they improve the standard of living for all.

Those who doubt the benefits of free trade highlight America's seemingly permanent trade deficit and worry that the debt the nation is piling up makes us vulnerable to those to whom we owe money. They claim that America is no longer producing high-paying factory jobs and point to real wages that have been stagnant for most Americans for several decades. America, they believe, is falling behind other nations in industrial capacity, and its young people face a future of low-wage employment in service industries.

Such criticisms of free trade have largely been limited to commentators or a few politicians who represent areas whose industries have been hard hit by foreign competition. Such politicians are rare: Since the end of World War II, U.S. leaders and their policies have generally been in favor of increasing openness to trade. Yet in recent years the seemingly unbreakable elite consensus on free trade is beginning to display some erosion. Former U.S. Treasury official Paul Craig Roberts claims that the era of nearly costless flows of capital makes classical free-trade theory meaningless, as the theory was based on the assumption that capital was fixed for each country. He holds that, today, much so-called free trade is merely the search for the cheapest labor and has little to do with improving efficiency or benefitting from comparative advantage. Roberts has been joined by a few economists and politicians such as Senator Charles Schumer of New York. Schumer and Roberts wrote in the *New York Times*, "This is a very different world than [nineteenth-century economist David] Ricardo envisioned. When American companies replace domestic employees with lower-cost foreign workers in order to sell more cheaply in home markets, it seems hard to argue that this is the way free trade is supposed to work."

It is likely that the debate over trade will continue and even increase in intensity as developing countries such as India and China strive to increase their share of the global market. The following chapter presents viewpoints on the nature of free trade and its effect on the American economy.

*"The consensus on trade among elites is
no longer as firm as it used to be."*

Policy Elites Are Beginning
to Doubt the Benefits
of Free Trade

Robert A. Senser

*Robert A. Senser has served as a labor attaché in the United
States Foreign Service. He has written numerous articles on
workers' rights and trade for publications such as* Foreign Affairs *and the* Monthly Labor Review. *In the following viewpoint, Senser argues that the American public has traditionally
expressed more concern about free trade than those who are influential in making policy, but in recent years doubts about the
benefits of free trade have been expressed by elite economists as
well. Senser believes that a public debate about the future of
trade policy is necessary.*

As you read, consider the following questions:

1. According to the survey cited by Senser, does the United
States public support unrestricted free trade?

2. What does economist Joseph E. Stiglitz, as cited by the author, think about intellectual property protection?

3. According to former assistant treasury secretary Paul Roberts, as cited by Senser, how is the situation today different from classical "Ricardian" free trade?

A little-noticed poll conducted nationwide in January 2004 by the University of Maryland's Program on International Policy Alternatives [PIPA] reveals the division in American public opinion about major trade issues. For starters, in probing the public's overall views, the PIPA poll did not ask whether people are for or against free trade; instead, it sought their opinion on the "growth of international trade," providing not two, but three choices.

Mixed Feelings About Free Trade

Of the three choices, only 18 percent of respondents took the truly "anti–free trade" position, agreeing with the statement, "I do not support the growth of international trade because I think the costs will inevitably outweigh the benefits." The other two choices both began with "I support the growth of international trade in principle," but then branched off into two different positions. Only about 20 percent approved of "the way the U.S. is going about expanding international trade." Most of the respondents, 53 percent, support the growth of international trade "in principle" but were "not satisfied with the way the U.S. government is dealing with the effects of trade on American jobs, the poor in other countries, and the environment."

In short, judging from this survey, most Americans support expanding trade but favor changes in the U.S. government's trade-related policies. An indication of this is the approval they give to specific trade agreements. About half of those surveyed support the 10-year-old North American Free Trade Agreement [NAFTA] and its proposed extension through the Central American Free Trade Agreement and the Free Trade Area of the Americas. But many of the respondents, among both those who approve and those who disapprove of the agreements, express concern about whether those agreements, and U.S. policy in general, adequately address human rights (including worker rights). Nearly three out of four respondents held that "as we become more involved economically with another country . . . we should be more concerned about human rights in that country." Even more respondents (nine out of ten) said that U.S. corporations operating in other countries should be expected to abide by U.S. health and safety standards for workers. An overwhelming 93 percent said that international trade agreements should require minimum standards for working conditions and for environmental protection.

Public opinion alone, of course, does not determine public policy, especially when trade policy has two strong supports: a firm consensus among an elite of policy makers, degree-credentialed professionals and other leading opinion-makers, including those in respected think tanks in favor of free trade; and a governmental and intergovernmental structure that institutionalizes that consensus.

In the United States, which is the leading force in setting and maintaining the trade, has both of these supports. But something startling is happening. First, the consensus on trade among elites is no longer as firm as it used to be. Second, while the international network of trade institutions built under that consensus, from the U.S. Trade Representative on up to the World Trade Organization, is not in danger, some of its policies are being challenged as never before.

Concern over Unbalanced Agreements

Three leading and widely respected economists are expressing reservations. One is Joseph E. Stiglitz, the eminent economist who won the 2001 Nobel Prize for economics. Stiglitz argues in his latest book, *The Roaring Nineties*, that the United States has mismanaged the global economy. In a talk at the Carnegie Council of Ethics in International Affairs, Stiglitz expanded on this charge:

> At the end of the Cold War, the United States as the sole superpower had an opportunity and a responsibility to reshape the global economic order, to try to create an international economic order based on principles like social justice. . . . But we lacked a vision. The financial and commercial sector in the United States did have a vision. They might not believe in government having an active role, except when it advanced their interest. The active role they pushed for was to gain market access. . . . As a result we got some very unbalanced trade agreements.

Stiglitz's history of concern over "unbalanced" (i.e., unfair) public policies spans his career as both a scholar and as a policy maker. He served as a member and later chairman of the Council of Economic Advisors during the first [Bill] Clinton administration and then as chief economist and senior vice president of the World Bank. Seven years in Washington gave him an on-the-job education in how economic theories do not necessarily advance the common good in practice. Two important examples that Stiglitz often cites are the protection of intellectual property rights and the requirement for free movement of capital across borders.

Protecting Intellectual Property

Stiglitz recognizes that patents, copyrights and other intellectual property rights need a measure of cross-border protection. But at the behest of drug companies and over the objections of the Council of Economic Advisors during Stiglitz's tenure there, U.S. negotiators delivered overprotection. "Unlike trade liberalization, which, at least under some idealist (and somewhat unrealistic) conditions can make everyone better off, stronger intellectual property rights typically make some

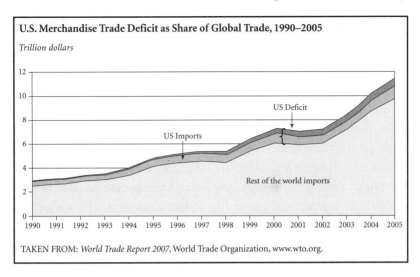

U.S. Merchandise Trade Deficit as Share of Global Trade, 1990–2005

Trillion dollars

US Deficit

US Imports

Rest of the world imports

TAKEN FROM: *World Trade Report 2007*, World Trade Organization, www.wto.org.

better off (the drug companies) and many worse off (those who otherwise might have been able to purchase the drugs)," Stiglitz writes in *The Roaring Nineties*.

Stiglitz is especially critical of the Clinton administration for launching a major change in the international development and trade system that requires countries to remove controls on the movement of financial capital across borders. He blames this policy for promoting global instability notably in the East Asian economic crisis of the 1990s, since it makes developing countries "subject to both the rational and irrational whims of the investor community, to their irrational exuberance and pessimism," as he wrote in *Globalization and Its Discontents*. . . . More recently, in a *New York Times* op-ed piece titled "The Broken Promise of NAFTA," Stiglitz warned against the plan to extend NAFTA's provision on capital mobility to Latin America, writing, "the International Monetary Fund has finally found such liberalization promotes neither growth nor stability in developing countries."

Another top-ranked economist, Jagdish Bhagwati, while championing globalization in his latest book, *In Defense of Globalization*, also attacks key elements of the trade consensus. Bhagwati, whom the Nobel laureate Robert Solow calls "our most powerful and persuasive advocate of free trade," expresses concerns that, surprisingly, he shares with Stiglitz: the overprotection of intellectual property rights and the unfettered flow of capital around the world.

Although he praises multinational corporations for the good they are doing, Bhagwati, by way of significant exception, condemns their "interest-driven lobbying" that caused the World Trade Organization [W.T.O.] to adopt unfair rules. He cites, as "a prime example," the U.S. pressure that led to the W.T.O. agreement on Trade-Related Aspects of Intellectual Property Rights [TRIPS]. "Pharmaceutical and software companies," he says, "muscled their way into the W.T.O. and turned it into a royalty-collection agency simply because the W.T.O. can apply trade sanctions" to violators of its rules. Unlike the legitimate trade responsibilities given the W.T.O. at its founding in 1994, TRIPS, in Bhagwati's view was like introducing "cancer cells into a healthy body," by which he meant that it "distorted and deformed an important multilateral institution, turning it away from its trade mission and rationale."

The "Wall Street–Treasury Complex"

Bhagwati has also been unrelenting in his attack on the pattern of removing restraints on cross-border capital mobility. In an essay titled "The Capital Myth," first published in *Foreign Affairs* in 1998 and now summarized in his latest book, Bhagwati argues that the unfettered flow of capital around the world is "inherently crisis-prone." Bhagwati blames a "power elite a la [sociologist] C. Wright Mills," "a definite network of like-minded luminaries among the powerful institutions— Wall Street, the Treasury Department, the State Department, the I.M.F. [International Monetary Fund] and the World Bank most prominent among them" for promulgating the myth that the unfettered flow of capital is a good thing. "This powerful network . . . is unable to look much beyond the interests of Wall Street, which it equates with the good of the world."

Bhagwati expresses satisfaction that both *The Economist* and the I.M.F. have lately lost their enthusiasm for free capital mobility, although "a watchful eye over the Wall Street–Treasury complex remains a necessity."

Thus two world-renowned economists, Stiglitz and Bhagwati, with very different perspectives on the state of today's global economy, have attacked the same key elements of the trade consensus still embraced by Washington (and still being pushed in current U.S. bilateral and regional trade negotiations).

Unexpectedly, that consensus is also under assault from a third economist, Paul Craig Roberts, former assistant secretary of the treasury in the [Ronald] Reagan administration and a former editor of *The Wall Street Journal*.

Roberts, whose long career in journalism and government service has been devoted to promoting free trade, now holds that the U.S. commitment to free trade is based on a "delusion" so serious that it threatens to turn the United States into a third world economy in 20 years. He disclosed his changed perspective earlier [in 2004] in three forums: a *New York Times* op-ed piece ("Second Thoughts about Free Trade," co-authored with New York's Democratic senator Charles Schumer), a Brookings Institution briefing, and a *Washington Post* interview.

"We all know free trade is good for us," he told the Brookings panel. "We've all learned this. [But] we live in the delusion that what is going on is free trade. It is not free trade."

Shifting Production Off-Shore

Roberts does not reject the fundamental economic principle of "comparative advantage" expounded in 1817 by the British economist David Ricardo. (The principle is explained as follows by the W.T.O.: "According to the principle of comparative advantage, the gains from trade follow from allowing an economy to specialize. For example, if a country is relatively better at making wine than wool, it makes sense to put more resources into wine, and to export some of the wine to pay for imports of wool.") Roberts argues, however, that comparative advantage is simply irrelevant; it doesn't apply today, two centuries after Ricardo and in a vastly different world. Why not? Ricardo's theory assumes that two major "factors of production"—labor and capital (factories, machinery)—cannot be moved off-shore; but today they can be, and this is being done on a massive scale.

"The way it's working today," he told *The Washington Post*'s Paul Blustein, "firms close facilities here, remove them to China, produce there, and send the products back here. This is not the Ricardian case for free trade." Moreover, now even labor effectively moves across borders as well, with Indian radiologists examining U.S. X-rays, for example, and Chinese software engineers writing computer codes. As a result, insists Roberts, "the case for free trade—that it benefits all countries—collapses." He predicts "tremendous dislocations, just as there were in the transformation out of feudalism to capitalism," because today's global economy makes it possible for multinational corporations, in their relentless search for lower costs and higher profits, to shift manufacturing and service operations to populous, labor-surplus countries like China and India.

Property Rights vs. Worker Rights

More and more American workers now see that happening to their jobs. Of course people do not own jobs, many economists argue; only capital—in the form of investments and other property, real and intellectual—confers true ownership, the type that merits active protection under the law. Protecting worker rights internationally is called protectionism; protecting property rights is not. But to large segments of the American public this distinction is meaningless. . . . America's elites, and even the general public, are starting to raise serious questions about America's free trade consensus.

| "In 1960, there were 54 million jobs in the United States; by 2004 there were 131 million."

Free Trade Has Led to More and Better Jobs in America

Russell Roberts

Russell Roberts is a professor of economics at George Mason University. He writes frequently on economics and trade for publications such as the Wall Street Journal *and the* New York Times. *In order to illustrate the benefits of free trade, Roberts has created an imaginary dialogue between a former owner of an American television factory, Ed Johnson, and the nineteenth-century theorist of free trade David Ricardo. The ghost of Ricardo has whisked Johnson away from an early 1960s debate about restricting imports of Japanese televisions. Ricardo explains how free trade benefits the future American economy despite the decline of domestic electronics manufacturing.*

As you read, consider the following questions:

1. According to Ricardo, what fringe benefits for American workers rose much more sharply than wages from 1960 to 2004?

2. According to this viewpoint, what is the major "cost" incurred by trying to grow your own food?

3. In Roberts's view, how would Ricardo respond to the statement, "Shutting factories destroys American jobs"?

"Can you prove that America is better off, Dave?"

"I would start with the evidence of your senses. The array of goods in that Circuit City store was pretty impressive, wasn't it?"

"Yes, it was. There was nothing like that back in 1960. Somebody must be buying those appliances and televisions."

"You could also look at your children and your workers' children and see that their standard of living is much higher than your generation's. But you don't know whether they are typical or not. To know what has happened to America overall, you must look at wages or income for most or all of the population."

"What do you find?"

"The government collects wage data for what it calls 'production or nonsupervisory workers.' They make up about 80 percent of the workforce. In 1960, the average worker in this group made $2.09 per hour. In 2004, the figure was $15.48 per hour."

"But what about inflation?"

"Good point, Ed. After taking into account higher prices, the seeming fivefold increase in wages was in fact 26 percent."

"Hmm. That's not a very impressive increase over almost 45 years."

"I agree. But there is a very misleading aspect of the comparison. In 2004, workers took much more of their income in the form of fringe benefits such as pension plans, health and dental insurance, and longer vacations. In fact, such forms of compensation more than doubled between 1960 and 2004.

The right measure of a worker's well-being should measure all forms of compensation, not just hourly wages."

"What happens when you account for the increase in fringe benefits?"

"The government has a survey of wages and benefits that covers a wider array of workers than just production and nonsupervisory workers. It's virtually everyone other than federal employees. Real hourly compensation for this larger group increased by more than 90 percent from 1960 to 2004. So it almost doubled. But the broadest measure of economic well-being would be per capita gross domestic product—"

"That's a mouthful."

"It is. But it is the broadest measure of how productive and wealthy we have become. After inflation, that number increased over 166 percent between 1960 and 2004, much more than double what it was before. And all of those estimates underestimate how much progress was made because of how hard it is to measure inflation accurately when the quality of the items, like those televisions we saw, is constantly improving."

"So America did well. But how could that be, Dave? What about unemployment? When we closed down our plant and Zenith and Motorola closed down theirs, America must have lost a lot of jobs."

"No. America just lost certain types of jobs. Do you like corn, Ed?"

"Yes, I do."

"Do you grow your own corn?"

"No."

"But you could, couldn't you? But you don't, for the same reason you don't do your own typing. It looks like growing your own corn is incredibly cheap. You just have the cost of a little seed. But growing your own corn is in fact incredibly expensive because of the time it takes to weed, water, and fertilize. That time appears to be free, but it is costly. You have lost the opportunity to earn money at some other activity and using that money to buy corn. Or having the time for leisure. If you think of your household as a nation, you import corn. You produce it in the roundabout way just like America produces televisions."

"But what if I were really good at growing corn?"

"Even if you were a fabulous farmer, it could be cheaper for you to work at something else and buy corn instead of growing it. It depends on whether it takes fewer minutes to grow an ear directly, or to earn enough money to buy corn by working at some other job using the roundabout way. You could say that your household has 'lost' the corn-growing job. But this would be a silly way of looking at what has occurred. You have lost the job of growing corn and gained a more valuable opportunity."

"What does that have to do with the jobs in the American television industry? Aren't they gone?"

"The television jobs are gone. But they have been replaced by other jobs. Think about agriculture. In 1900, about 40 percent of the American workforce was in agriculture. By the end of the twentieth century, that number was under 3 percent. The proportion of the workforce needed to feed the American people fell dramatically, not because of imports but because of better technology. But did that technology cost America jobs? It cost America certain types of jobs, but the overall number of jobs increased tremendously."

"But didn't those farming jobs disappear, Dave?"

"Not in the way you'd think. A farmer didn't wake up one morning to find his overalls gone, his tractor vanished, and his fields of grain replaced by a shopping center. As technology improved, some farmers' incomes fell. Some farmers retired early. Others sold their farms to more efficient farmers. And some just struggled until retirement. But the biggest change caused by that technology was invisible. The dreams of the children of farmers changed. Those children saw that agriculture was not a booming industry. Even though their parents and grandparents had been farmers, they saw that farming was going to be less profitable than it had been. Some of them weren't thrilled about becoming farmers, anyway. They made plans to become salespeople, engineers, chemists, and pilots. And those jobs were available precisely because America made the decision to let the agricultural sector get smaller."

"You're saying that the people took different types of jobs."

"That's right. Some even went into a new industry called television. Can you imagine how poor America would be in 1960 or 2005 if America had made a decision back in 1900 to preserve the size of the farming industry in the name of saving jobs?"

"But the agriculture jobs we lost went to other Americans. It's not like we started importing food."

"What's the difference?"

"I don't know. It seems like the two cases ought to be different. When American farmers lose their jobs because other Americans figure out a new technology, at least the inventors who benefit are Americans. When American farmers lose their jobs because foreigners sell food to America more cheaply, the benefits go to foreigners."

"In fact, either way makes America better off."

"How?"

"In either case, America gets less expensive food with a smaller number of farmers. That is the important change. You see America losing jobs. I see Americans spending less on food—food is cheaper, and fewer Americans have to work in the food business. American consumers are better off. But so are most American workers. When consumers have less expensive food, they have more resources to spend on other things. Industries other than farming can now expand. And they can find workers because not as many Americans are needed to grow food. This allows Americans to make more of other things now that they don't have to make as much food.

David Ricardo: Economic Theorist

David Ricardo (1772–1823) was an English stockbroker who, working at the beginning of the nineteenth century, emerged as a major economic thinker during the early years of the industrial revolution. He is often referred to as the founder of scientific economics, because he used mathematics and abstract examples in his writing. . . .

Ricardo's approach to economics was new. Before him, economic writing was more literary than scientifically precise. . . . Ricardo chose to write about economics in a concise way, by eliminating numerous examples and instead explaining his ideas about the economy by using simple, easy-to-understand abstract models. Pursuing economic theory as a science, he explored economics by using basic principles and deductive reasoning to work toward his conclusions.

Gale Encyclopedia of U.S. Economic History, *1999.*

Let me ask you a question, Ed. Do you think it would be good for America if all disease disappeared and everyone were perfectly healthy until the age of 120?"

"Sure."

"Why do you answer so quickly? Aren't you worried about what would happen to the doctors? America would lose all those high-paying doctor and health care jobs."

"Oh come on, Dave. If we could get rid of disease, doctors shouldn't stand in the way. They would just have to find other things to do."

"And if America finds a cheaper way to make televisions by importing them?"

"It's just not the same. Cheaper televisions are not as important as getting rid of disease."

"But the principle is the same. Would a doctor have a right to force a person to stay sick so the doctor could continue earning the living the doctor was accustomed to? Does a television manufacturer have the right to force a consumer of televisions to pay a higher price to sustain high wages for his workers? But perhaps these are issues for a philosopher. In any case, we don't lose jobs if we eliminate disease or if foreigners sell America inexpensive televisions. Certain types of jobs are lost. If disease disappeared, we'd lose the medical jobs. People who would have been doctors would now apply their skills to other activities and enrich our lives and their own. Paradoxically, America would lose the high-paying jobs in health care but still become wealthier."

"And what about the people who are already doctors?"

"They would suffer hardship. The size of that hardship would depend on how disease disappeared. If it happened slowly, the hardship would be less, and medical workers would have time to adjust. If it happened literally overnight, it would be a lot crueler—to the doctors anyway. The sick would rather see disease disappear quickly."

"But when a factory closes, doesn't America have fewer jobs?"

"Just fewer jobs in that industry. The overall number of jobs in the United States exploded between 1960 and the end of the century. In 1960, there were 54 million jobs in the United States. By 2004, there were 131 million."

"Wow. That is amazing."

"Don't be misled. The ultimate reason jobs expanded was that the United States population was expanding, and a higher percentage of that population, particularly women, wanted to work. But the key point is that there were jobs for that expanded population, even though a lot of traditional American industries such as electronics, automobiles, and steel are smaller or have disappeared."

> *"Free trade does to a nation what alcohol does to a man: saps him first of his vitality, then his energy, then his independence, then his life."*

Free Trade Is Killing American Industry

Patrick J. Buchanan

Patrick J. Buchanan is a well-known conservative commentator and the author of books such as The Great Betrayal *and* The Death of the West. *Buchanan notes America's long history of protectionism in the following viewpoint. He compares the free-trading Great Britain of the late eighteenth century to the protectionist United States of the same period, noting that free-trading Britain—the world-dominating manufacturing power— declined, while the United States followed the protectionist vision of Alexander Hamilton to become an industrial dynamo. Today, according to Buchanan, the United States is in the same position as Great Britain was a century and a half ago.*

As you read, consider the following questions:

1. How did Alexander Hamilton propose to help industry in the newly independent United States, according to Buchanan?

2. According to the author, how much of the U.S. gross national product was exported at the start of World War I?

3. In Buchanan's opinion, what are the two major noneconomic losses the United States has suffered in order to pursue free trade?

Across America the story is the same: steel and lumber mills going into bankruptcy; textile plants moving to the Caribbean, Mexico, Central America, and the Far East; auto plants closing and opening overseas; American mines being sealed and farms vanishing. Seven hundred thousand textile workers—many of them minorities and single women—have lost their jobs since NAFTA [North American Free Trade Agreement] passed in 1993.

Three Decades of Free Trade

Thirty years have elapsed since our free-trade era began and 30 months [as of August 2003] since George W. Bush became president. It's time to measure the promise of global free trade against the performance.

Undeniably, free trade has delivered for consumers. A trip to the mall, where the variety of suits, shoes, shirts, toys, gadgets, games, TVs, and appliances abounds, makes the case. But what has it cost our country?

Every month George Bush has been in office, America has lost manufacturing jobs. One in seven has vanished since his inauguration. In 1950, a third of our labor force was in manufacturing. Now, it is 12.5 percent. U.S. manufacturing is in a death spiral, and it is not a natural death. This is a homicide. Open-borders free trade is killing American manufacturing.

In 2002, we ran a trade deficit in goods of $484 billion. This May [2003], it reached the level of $562 billion, nearly 6 percent of GDP [gross domestic product]. Evangelists of free trade tell us trade deficits do not matter. Michael Boskin, chairman of the Council of Economic Advisers under Bush I [George H.W. Bush], declared, "It does not make any difference whether a country makes computer chips or potato chips."

History teaches otherwise. In 1860, Britain abandoned its Britain First trade policy for the free-trade faith of [nineteenth-century British economists] David Ricardo, John Stuart Mill, and Richard Cobden. By World War I, Britain, which produced twice what America did in 1860, produced less than half and had been surpassed by a Germany that did not even exist in 1860.

Free trade does to a nation what alcohol does to a man: saps him first of his vitality, then his energy, then his independence, then his life.

The Importance of Manufacturing

America today exhibits the symptoms of a nation passing into late middle age. We spend more than we earn. We consume more than we produce.

Why does it matter where our goods are produced? Because, as I wrote in *The Great Betrayal*:

> Manufacturing is the key to national power. Not only does it pay more than service industries, the rates of productivity growth are higher and the potential of new industries arising is far greater. From radio came television, VCRs, and flat-panel screens. From adding machines came calculators and computers. From the electric typewriter came the word processor. Research and development follow manufacturing.

Alexander Hamilton, the architect of the U.S. economy, knew this. He had served in the Revolution as aide to [George] Washington and lived through the British blockades. He had led the bayonet charge at Yorktown. And he had resolved that never again would his country's survival depend upon French muskets or French ships.

As first treasury secretary, he delivered in 1791 the "Report on Manufactures," one of America's great state papers. Reflecting on how close his country had come to losing its liberty, Hamilton wrote,

> Not only the wealth, but the independence and security of a country, appear to be materially connected with the prosperity of manufactures. Every nation. . . ought to endeavor to possess within itself all the essentials of a national supply. These comprise the means of subsistence, habitation, clothing and defense.

Under the Constitution he helped write, a national free-trade zone was created. Hamilton's idea was to use tariffs to end our dependence on Europe and force British merchants to finance our government and the roads, harbors, and canals that would tie America together with commerce.

Tariffs would give our national government the revenue to operate, while providing our people both privileged access to the fastest growing market on earth and incentives to go into manufacturing. With American manufacturing thus encouraged, we would soon produce ourselves the guns and ships to defend the republic and the necessities of our national life so we could stand alone against the world.

Protectionism Helped America Grow

For 12 decades, America followed Hamilton's vision. On the eve of World War I, the 13 agricultural colonies on the eastern seaboard had become the richest nation on earth with the highest standard of living, a republic that produced 96 percent of all it consumed while exporting 8 percent of its GNP [gross national product], an industrial colossus that manufactured more than Britain, France, and Germany combined.

The self-sufficiency and industrial power Hamiltonian policies created enabled us to rearm in security, crush the Axis [Powers who started World War I] in four years, rebuild Europe and Japan, and outlast the Soviet empire in a Cold War, while meeting all the needs of our people.

But in the Clinton-Bush free-trade era, Alexander Hamilton is derided as a "protectionist." [U.S. president] Woodrow Wilson's free-trade dogma is gospel. Result: our trade surpluses have vanished, our deficits have exploded, our self-sufficiency has been lost, our sovereignty has been diminished, and an industrial base that was the envy of mankind has been gutted.

And for what? All that junk down at the mall? What do we have now that we did not have before we submitted to this cult of free trade?

The Loss of Independence

Consider the depths of our new dependency. Imports, 4 percent of GDP for the first 70 years of the 20th century, are near 15 percent now, and 30 percent of the manufactures we consume. Pat Choate, author of *Agents of Influence*, gives the following levels of U.S. dependency on foreign suppliers for critical goods:

- Medicines and pharmaceuticals: 72 percent

- Metalworking machinery: 51 percent

- Engines and power equipment: 56 percent

- Computer equipment: 70 percent

- Communications equipment: 67 percent

- Semiconductors and electronics: 64 percent

In July [2003], the U.S. Business and Industrial Council reported that the Pentagon officials responsible for procuring U.S. weapons had joined with defense industries to oppose legislation requiring 65 percent U.S. content. U.S. missile defense and the Joint Strike Fighter would be imperiled if 65 percent of the components had to be made in the USA.

Sharp Decline in U.S. Manufacturing Jobs

Over the past five years [2001–2006] the US economy experienced a net job loss in goods-producing activities. The entire job growth was in service-providing activities—primarily credit intermediation, health care and social assistance, waiters, waitresses and bartenders, and state and local government.

US manufacturing lost 2.9 million jobs, almost 17 percent of the manufacturing workforce. The wipeout is across the board. Not a single manufacturing payroll classification created a single new job.

Paul Craig Roberts,
Baltimore Chronicle & Sentinel, *February 13, 2006.*

As Choate writes, Dell Computers of Austin [Texas] has 4,500 suppliers. Its just-in-time supply line, which stretches across the Atlantic and Pacific, has an inventory of four days. A dock strike on either coast, and Dell begins to close down after 96 hours.

The Loss of Sovereignty

In the lame-duck session of Congress after the GOP [Republican Party] triumph of 1994, [former Senate leader] Bob Dole and [former House Speaker] Newt Gingrich colluded with [President Bill] Clinton to bring us into a World Trade Organization [WTO] where we are outvoted 15–1 by the European Union [EU]. In its most important ruling, the WTO has held that the foreign sales corporations of U.S. exporters like Microsoft and Boeing, set up to receive tax benefits voted by Congress, violate the rules of free trade.

Europe is now authorized to impose $4 billion in tariff penalties on U.S. exports if Congress fails to rewrite our tax laws to conform to WTO commands.

When America bailed out the world in the Asian crisis of 1997–98, Indonesia, South Korea, Russia, and Brazil devalued their currencies, slashing the dollar price of their exports. To enable them to earn the hard currency to pay back Western banks and the IMF [International Monetary Fund], America agreed to keep her markets open. Soon, steel from Indonesia, South Korea, Japan, Russia, and Brazil was being dumped in the United States, and American mills were reeling.

The recent steel decision is instructive. By 2002, 25 steel companies had gone bankrupt, and the International Trade Commission had identified dumping as the industry killer. Invoking U.S. trade law, President Bush imposed tariffs. The dumpers howled and ran to the WTO, which declared the U.S. tariffs unjustified. Either the Congress removes them or the EU is empowered to impose $2 billion in tariff penalties on U.S. exports.

Consider what submission to the WTO has meant. Our Congress is ordered by foreign bureaucrats to alter U.S. law or our companies face penalties. Presidential decisions to protect vital American industries are declared invalid by Eurocrats. The terms of access to the U.S. market are now to be decided in Geneva [Switzerland] by Lilliputians of the New World Order.

Why Are We Letting This Happen?

Libertarians teach that free trade provides a check on government power. By enabling citizens to buy outside their borders, free trade forces governments to reduce regulations and taxes to stay competitive.

A fine theory. Has it worked out? Hardly. History shows that the opposite is true. [German leader Otto von] Bismarck's *Zollverein*, or customs union, went hand-in-hand with the rise of the Second Reich. The EU evolved from a free-trade common market into the socialist superstate of today that is the model for the world government under which all nations surrender sovereignty and how we live will be decided by Platonic guardians.

In the protectionist era from 1789 to 1933, U.S. taxes rarely took more than 3 percent of GNP, except in wartime. Government relied on tariffs. Before 1913, except for the Civil War era and briefly under [President Grover] Cleveland, we had no income tax. But in the free-trade era, U.S. tax rates on incomes, currently 35 percent, have risen as high as 70 percent, and spending has exceeded 20 percent of GDP in peacetime. The free-trade era is the era of Big Government.

As a former Friedmanite [adherent of economist Milton Friedman] free trader, let me say it: free trade is a bright shining lie. Free trade is the Trojan Horse of world government. Free trade is the murderer of manufacturing and the primrose path to the loss of national sovereignty and the end of our independence.

> "In truth, the overall effect of trade on
> the number of jobs in an economy is
> best approximated as zero."

Free Trade Helps Working Americans

Douglas Irwin

In the following viewpoint, Douglas Irwin, a professor of economics at Dartmouth College and author of Free Trade Under Fire, *describes how trade fits into the dynamic nature of the American economy. Change is constantly happening—some businesses fail while new ones take their place, he argues. In a free-trade system, Irwin maintains, American labor and capital will flow to those industries in which the United States is more efficient, while other industries will lose out to foreign competition. Irwin asserts that the ultimate impact of free trade on the number of jobs is minimal.*

As you read, consider the following questions:

1. What did populists of a century ago believe about free trade, according to Irwin?

Douglas Irwin, "Does International Trade Kill Good American Jobs?" *American Enterprise*, June 2004, pp. 31–33. Copyright © 2004 American Enterprise Institute for Public Policy Research. Reproduced with permission of The American Enterprise, a national magazine of Politics, Business, and Culture (TAEmag.com).

2. How can the author claim that the overall—or net—effect on jobs in the United States is zero?

3. What is one example that Irwin uses to show how import protections for one American industry are hurting another industry?

In 1824 the great British historian Thomas Macaulay remarked that "free trade, one of the greatest blessings which a government can confer on a people, is in almost every country unpopular." The popularity of free trade has not changed much since Macaulay's day. The 1990s were a period of expanding world trade, strong economic growth, and the lowest U.S. unemployment in 30 years. Yet the decade began with fears of the "giant sucking sound" of jobs lost due to the North American Free Trade Agreement (NAFTA), and ended with opponents of free trade taking to the streets in the "Battle of Seattle."

Perennial Complaints About Free Trade

While free trade has always been the subject of complaint, the rhetorical charges against it have stepped up in recent years. Critics like Ralph Nader and Pat Buchanan rail against international commerce and the World Trade Organization for serving the interests of corporations rather than people, harming workers, decimating manufacturing industries, weakening environmental protections, and undermining American sovereignty. A wide range of groups, from religious organizations to human rights activists to Greens, have joined in the protests. The litany of complaints placed on the doorstep of free trade is hugely extensive, going well beyond the perennial objection that trade forces painful economic adjustments such as plant closings and layoffs. Nader charges that free trade "would make the air you breathe dirtier, and the water you drink more polluted. It would cost jobs, depress wage levels, and make workplaces less safe. It would destroy family farms and undermine consumer protections."

Ironically, it was the inequities of *protectionism* that populists railed against a century ago. They warned that big businesses used tariffs to stifle competition and exploit consumers. They argued that free trade was the best way to ensure competition, discipline the power of domestic monopolies, and prevent politicians from using tariffs to give favors to special interests.

The clear conclusion of economists of all stripes is that the populists of a hundred years ago were right, and the populists of today are wrong. Free trade is a desirable economic policy for the "little man" at least as much as for the national economy. This conclusion is supported by extensive empirical evidence. Yet protectionism is far from vanquished in the political arena.

Trade Increases Overall Employment

Industries that compete against imports will always promote their own interests by seeking trade restrictions. But today, the general public also has concerns about foreign competition. The argument that resonates most strongly is the claim that imports destroy jobs. Is this accurate? And if so, are import restrictions the remedy?

The claim that trade should be limited because imports destroy jobs has been trotted out since the sixteenth century. And imports do indeed destroy jobs in certain industries. Employment in the Maine shoe industry and the South Carolina apparel industry, for example, is lower because both industries were exposed to competition from imports. So we can understand why the plant owners and workers and politicians who represent them might prefer to avoid this foreign competition.

But just because imports destroy some jobs does not mean that trade reduces overall employment or harms the economy. After all, the dollars that U.S. consumers hand over to other countries in purchasing imports do not accumulate there. Those dollars, as an economic fact, must eventually all return to purchase either U.S. goods (exports) or U.S. assets (foreign investment). And both exports and foreign investment create new jobs here.

The claim that imports destroy jobs ignores the creation of jobs elsewhere in the economy as a result of trade. Since trade both destroys *and* creates jobs, the pertinent question is whether trade has a *net* effect on employment. In truth, the overall effect of trade on the number of jobs in an economy is best approximated as zero. That's because total employment is not a function of international trade, but of the number of people in the labor force. Historical data show clearly that the number of jobs in the United States closely tracks the number of people who are available to work. That is to be expected in a free-market economy. Any imbalance in the numbers of workers and jobs will be offset by an adjustment of wages or some other change in economic equilibrium.

Imports and Exports Related

The same adjustments apply in trade. Some participants in the trade debate imagine that a country's exports and imports are independent of one another, and that we ought to strive to reduce imports while increasing exports. But in truth, you can't reduce one without having an adverse effect on the other—for exports and imports are flip sides of the same coin. You can't have one without the other.

The mechanisms that link a country's exports and imports to one another are complex and not always readily apparent, but they can be illustrated by focusing on the foreign exchange market. If the United States unilaterally reduces its tariffs on Japanese goods, for example, one would expect U.S. demand for Japanese goods to increase. To make these purchases, consumers in the United States will (indirectly) have to sell dollars on the foreign exchange market to purchase yen. In response to the increased demand for yen from those holding dollars, the value of the dollar will fall compared to yen. That raises the price of Japanese goods in the United States, dampening demand for those goods.

And there is a flip side: Even though it was the United States that lowered its tariff while Japan left its tariffs unchanged, Japan will now purchase more goods from the United States. This is because the cheaper dollar lowers the yen price of U.S. goods, stimulating Japanese demand for them. Economic statistics going back more than a century document this sort of direct link between outgoing and incoming trade.

The foreign exchange market is just one of several mechanisms that link exports and imports. And together, these mechanisms ensure that exports and imports, rather than being separate forces, one "good" and one "bad," are actually related phenomena that rise and fall together. Indeed, the best way to think of exports may be as goods that a country must give up in order to acquire the imports it desires. Economically, both imports and exports are good for an economy and for consumers.

Restricting Imports Hurts Jobs

This is why, throughout U.S. history, large tariff increases that choke off imports have failed to stimulate greater employment. Any increase in employment in import-competing industries is offset by a decrease in employment in export-oriented industries. The Smoot-Hawley tariff of 1930, for example, significantly reduced imports but failed to create jobs overall because exports fell almost one-for-one with imports, resulting in employment losses in those industries.

The connection between imports and exports cannot be overlooked when evaluating trade policy. Governments that undertake policies to reduce imports will find themselves reducing exports also. That merely trades one expansion for another contraction, and both transactions will end up being done less efficiently.

Free Trade Has Helped U.S. Growth

During the 50-plus years under GATT [General Agreement on Tariffs and Trade] (and later the WTO), trade barriers have been reduced substantially, with a commensurate increase in global economic growth both in developed countries and in developing countries that embraced trade liberalization. The United States and its citizens have overwhelmingly benefited from this policy, which has paved the way for six decades of economic expansion and increased living standards. Some specifics are:

- The average U.S. tariff rate on all goods has fallen from over 19 percent in 1933 to 1.6 percent in 2003. The tariff rate on dutiable imports has fallen from nearly 60 percent to 4.9 percent today.

- Trade (as a percentage of the GDP [gross domestic product]) has climbed from single digits in the 1930s to nearly one-quarter of the U.S. GDP in 2003.

- During this period of increased trade liberalization and reliance on trade, real per capita GDP in the U.S. (in constant 2000 dollars) has climbed from a low of $5,061 in 1933 to $35,726 in 2003.

Edwin Feulner et al., Heritage Foundation, August 10, 2004.

Not only do import restrictions reduce the number of jobs producing exports. They also directly destroy jobs in downstream industries that use imports. Keep in mind that the majority of U.S. imports are not final consumer goods, but intermediate goods used by domestic firms in their production processes. Any trade restriction that raises the price of an intermediate good directly harms downstream user industries, and this adversely affects employment in those industries.

Restrictions on imported sugar, for example, have reduced U.S. employment in the sugar refining and candy making industries. Because our food manufacturers who produce sugar-intensive products must pay a higher price for sweetener than their foreign rivals, their competitive position has suffered. In 1990, Brachs Candy Company announced that due to the high domestic price of sugar it would close a factory in Chicago that employed 3,000 workers and expand production instead in Canada—which does not artificially inflate the price of sugar to protect its sugar producers. In 1988, the Department of Commerce estimated that the high price of domestic sugar due to U.S. protectionism cost almost 9,000 jobs in food manufacturing because of increased imports of cheaper sugar-containing products, and 3,000 jobs in the sugar-refining industry because of lower demand for sugar. At the time of this study, U.S. sugar-producing farms employed about 35,000 workers—but the sugar-processing and sugar-using sectors employed about 708,000 workers! A great many workers in the sugar-using industries were put at risk, in other words, to save the jobs of the few workers in the sugar-producing industry.

Less Desirable Jobs

We have seen that framing trade policy in terms of employment is ultimately an empty exercise. Blocking imports may protect some jobs, but it harms others. Yet even those who agree that the overall effect of trade on employment is essentially zero may oppose free trade because they believe that it shifts jobs into *less desirable* sectors. The gravest of such concerns is that in the last three decades good jobs in manufacturing have been traded for bad jobs of other sorts. Has trade actually had this effect on the U.S.?

The economics reveal that the popular perception that imports destroy good, high-wage jobs in manufacturing is almost completely erroneous. It is closer to the truth to say that imports destroy bad, low-wage jobs in manufacturing.

This is because wages in industries that compete against imports are well below average, whereas wages in exporting industries are well above average. The United States tends to import labor-intensive products, such as apparel, footwear, leather, and goods assembled from components. U.S. companies in these labor-intensive sectors tend to employ workers with lower than average educational attainment and relatively low wages. In 1999, average hourly earnings of Americans working in the apparel industry were 36 percent less than in manufacturing as a whole. Average hourly earnings were 30 percent lower than average in the leather industry and 23 percent lower in the textile industry.

By contrast, the products the United States tends to export are more skill-intensive, such as aircraft, construction machinery, engines and turbines, and industrial chemicals. Workers in these industries earn relatively high wages. In 1999, average hourly earnings in the aircraft industry were 42 percent above the average in manufacturing. Wages were 8 percent higher in industrial machinery, and 24 percent higher in pharmaceuticals. One study reports that even "after being adjusted for skill differences, wages in export-intensive industries are 11 percent above average, whereas wages in import-intensive industries are 15 percent below average."

As a result, any policy that limits overall trade by reducing exports and imports tends to increase U.S. employment in low-wage industries and reduce U.S. employment in high-wage industries. Restricting trade shifts American workers away from things that they produce well (and hence export and earn high wages in producing), and toward things that they do not produce so well (and hence import and earn low wages in producing). Under trade restrictions, employment gains for low-wage textile factory operators would be offset by employment losses for high-wage machinists and engineers in aircraft and pharmaceutical plants.

Free Trade Helps Average Workers

In any rapidly changing economy, jobs are continuously created and eliminated. Changes in consumer tastes, domestic competition, growth in productivity, technological innovation, and international trade all contribute to the churning of the labor market. It is virtually impossible to disentangle all of the reasons for job displacement because they are interdependent; for example, technological change may be stimulated by domestic or foreign competition.

Yet to the extent that such attributions can be made, the available economic evidence suggests that trade is a small factor in the displacement of American workers. According to the Bureau of Labor Statistics, import competition was responsible for only 1.5 percent of total layoffs from 1996 to 1999. And counterbalancing this, as we have seen, are many positive effects on workers from unshackled trade.

Free trade, it is clear, is not only very good for economies and for consumers. It is also good for the average American worker.

| *"In this supercharged world of foreign-bought and corporate-owned influence, ordinary Americans don't get much of a hearing."*

A Free Trade-Oriented Elite Is Betraying American Workers

Sherrod Brown

Sherrod Brown is a United States Senator from Ohio. Previously he served in the House of Representatives (elected 1992) where he was known as a leader in the opposition to trade agreements such as the Central American Free Trade Agreement (CAFTA). In this viewpoint, taken from his book Myths of Free Trade, *Brown puts the blame for the loss of high-wage industrial jobs on the rise of a globally oriented elite. Corporate chief executive officers (CEOs), columnists, and former politicians, Brown argues, press for treaties like GATT (the General Agreement on Tariffs and Trade) and NAFTA (the North American Free Trade Agreement). Brown asserts that some current and former American politicians have been bought by foreign countries interested in opening the United States' market to their products, while others genuinely—if wrongly—believe in the benefits of free trade. For American workers, the devotion of the elite members of society to free trade has often meant loss of high-paying factory jobs, the author maintains.*

As you read, consider the following questions:

1. What method do corporations and foreign companies use to get politicians to pass favorable legislation, according to Brown?
2. According to the author, how many steel production jobs were lost in 2001?
3. How did the executives of the LTV steel company benefit from plant closures, according to Brown?

From 1979 to 1994, registered foreign agents—American citizens representing foreign concerns and lobbying the U.S. Congress or executive branch—increased eightfold! Since then the numbers have continued to grow, and it is not only foreign countries these lobbyists represent. Literally thousands of American attorneys, former government officials, former congressmen and senators, and others represent American corporations that are doing business abroad and foreign companies doing business in the United States and looking for special treatment from Congress.

The Steel Crisis

In this supercharged world of foreign-bought and corporate-owned influence, ordinary Americans don't get much of a hearing. Consider the case of steel. Every country that wants to be a player in the world economy has its own steel industry. Many subsidize it. Most export to the United States as much as possible. November 1998 steel imports into the United States, for example, increased 72 percent over imports one year earlier. Total imports in November 1998 were 37 percent of U.S. steel consumption, the highest on record; historically it stood at about 20 percent. Total 1998 steel imports were almost one-third higher than those in 1997, which itself was a record-setting year. Andrew Sharkey III, American Iron and Steel Institute (AISI) president and CEO, declared that "the U.S. remains the World's Steel Dumping Ground."

Tens of thousands of steelworker jobs were in peril. Thousands marched on Washington throughout 1998 and 1999. At least a score of congressmen and congresswomen from steel districts spoke out and introduced legislation. Speakers at rallies in Ohio, Indiana, Illinois, West Virginia, Pennsylvania, and Alabama—America's preeminent steelmaking states—were demanding help.

Hardest hit may have been the Ohio Valley in eastern Ohio and northern West Virginia. Fear of the future, a sentiment all too well known in this part of America, filled the air in the Ohio River towns of Steubenville, Ohio, and Weirton, West Virginia. Every recession and economic downturn that afflicted America in the last quarter-century hit the Ohio Valley especially hard. But this one seemed worse. Almost a quarter of Weirton Steel's 4,000 employees had been laid off by November 1998. While the rest of America was prospering (or at least that's what Ohio Valley residents saw on television, and that's what the president had told the nation), to these steelworkers, the future looked no better than the already bleak present.

Rich Littleton, one of the laid-off steelworkers, sat in the union hall in Weirton in 1999 and lamented to *Columbus Dispatch* reporters Ron Carter and Jonathan Riskind, "I'm 38 years old. How marketable am I? This used to be something you could count on. I always wanted to do the same thing my father did. It scares me that I might not be able to give to my family the same things this place gave to me."

In 1984 the community and the employees of Weirton Steel saved the plant when they put together an Employee Stock Ownership Plan (ESOP), cut the administrative fat at the factory, and invested in new equipment and state-of-the-art technology. Rich Littleton's father and both his grandfathers had worked in the mill. Littleton's wife also worked in the mill. Weirton Steel laid her off along with her husband. Their combined annual income had approached $70,000; now they had no idea about their future. "You don't know from one moment to the next whether you're going to be able to put food on the table or pay the rent. . . . This is what we know. This is what we do." In early 2004 ISG [International Steel Group] bought a bankrupt Weirton Steel.

Seeking Help from Washington

The steel crisis put U.S. steel executives in a difficult position. They excoriated the president [Bill Clinton] and [Clinton administration] Secretary of the Treasury Robert Rubin for their refusal to address the impending loss of jobs in their industry. In early 1999, as the crisis deepened, steel executives fanned out to Capitol Hill offices, imploring members of Congress to help. They asked for congressional pressure on the president, political pressure on the vice president, and legislative action from us [Congress]. One prominent Republican steel executive from Ohio came to my office and said, "Tell your friend Al Gore that he needs us, that he needs Ohio to win the election next year, and that he better step up to the plate."

Steel executives felt betrayed by a president who was now, in their minds, dead wrong on trade. Until the steel crisis, however, they thought the president was consistently right on trade—on NAFTA [North American Free Trade Agreement], on GATT [General Agreement on Tariffs and Trade], on trade with China, and on Fast Track [procedures adopted by the U.S. Congress to expedite the passage of international trade agreements]. Ironically, a stubborn consistency from a free trade president now mystified them. And a business class consistently on the wrong side—and a political class that refused to fight for fair trade—cost thousands of steelworkers their livelihoods.

In 2001 the problem grew markedly worse. Nationally, more than two dozen steel companies had declared bankruptcy since the crisis began three years earlier. Close to 50,000 jobs were lost. In northeast Ohio three steel companies filed for bankruptcy, jeopardizing at least 12,000 jobs. LTV, the third-largest integrated steel company in the United States, shut its doors, throwing 3,000 people out of work. On March 31, 2002, 45,000 retirees lost their health benefits. Retirees also feared that part of their pensions would be jeopardized. Congressional reaction was swift, until Republican leadership stopped dead in its tracks any legislative action.

Bush Administration Policy

Vice presidential candidate [Dick] Cheney had promised in Wheeling, West Virginia, in October 2000 that he and George W. Bush would not sit idly by as America's steel industry crumbled. As bankruptcies mounted during Bush's first year in office, and as more than one million industrial jobs were lost, the pressure on the administration to act built rapidly. Bush invoked Section 201 of the Trade Act of 1974—a mechanism to set the stage for an investigation of unfair trade practices that would allow the president to slap significant tariffs on illegal dumped steel. But despite the warnings of United Steelworkers president Leo Girard and the CEOs of America's steel companies, the president hesitated in the early days of 2002, delaying the decision on whether to implement the tariffs. LTV idled its mills, and as LTV workers lost jobs, incomes, pensions, and health benefits, LTV executives reaped a bonanza. In a harbinger of things to come—a sort of Enron conservatism in which executives enrich themselves as they and market forces destroy companies—LTV's top executives gave themselves bonuses of several million dollars. Finally, the president did place significant tariffs on imported steel, giving some breathing room to the beleaguered industry but less

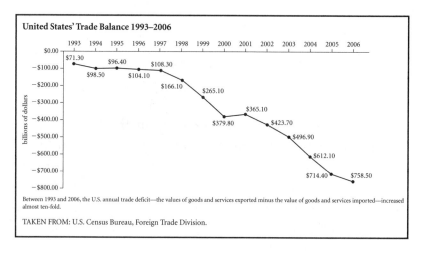

United States' Trade Balance 1993–2006

Between 1993 and 2006, the U.S. annual trade deficit—the values of goods and services exported minus the value of goods and services imported—increased almost ten-fold.

TAKEN FROM: U.S. Census Bureau, Foreign Trade Division.

than the industry thought was needed. President Bush then allowed the tariff to expire, devastating steel executives and workers.

There is little loyalty on the part of many corporations to the communities in which their executives live and the country that they call home. The late Robert Bartley, head cheerleader for free trade's chief cheering squad, the *Wall Street Journal*, said hopefully, "I think the nation-state is finished." Former Clinton Labor Secretary Robert Reich said more sympathetically, "Gone is the tight connection between the company, its community, even its country. Vanishing too are the paternalistic corporate heads who used to feel a sense of responsibility for their local community. Emerging in their place is the new global manager." A spokesman for Union Carbide intoned: "It is not proper for an international corporation to put the welfare of any country in which it does business above that of any other." Those somber statements, of course, do not stop them from petitioning Congress for special tax advantages as American companies, lobbying for government contracts, asking American regulators for special dispensation, playing to American patriotism in their advertising, or even declaring their loyalty to the Cleveland Indians baseball team when advertising in Cleveland.

Unfettered Global Capitalism

President George W. Bush, always on the side of America's most powerful corporations, set the tone of his administration in 2001 when he quietly delayed, then reversed, a new policy that blocked government contracts for companies that had defrauded the government. Law and order, apparently, only goes so far with conservative politicians.

The new global captains of industry assure us that if they can operate without interference from national governments, they will provide the capital and jobs to create huge, vibrant middle classes in dozens of developing countries. They tell us repeatedly to get out of the way. Without the burden of environmental rules and labor standards, they can lift hundreds of millions of people out of poverty. These corporations, obviously powerful forces in the media (which they own) and government (which they seem to lease), have convinced their countries to adopt economic policies that, as billionaire financier and European Parliament member Sir James Goldsmith said, "makes you rich if you eliminate your national workforce and transfer production abroad, and which bankrupts you if you continue to employ your own people." Stanley Mihelick, executive vice president of Goodyear, commented, "Until we get real wages down much closer to those of the Brazils and Koreas, we cannot pass along productivity gains to wages and still be competitive." Former General Electric CEO Jack Welch found the best way to chase cheap labor was to "have every plant you own on a barge."

Elite Resents Democratic Government

The economic titans will continue to play off government against government, further weakening environmental and food safety standards in both nations, sapping governments' ability to govern, and unraveling our own system of self-government. Interference by government—as the most sophisticated among the world's elite keep telling us—is inefficient, problematic, and simply unnatural. Unshackle business. Allow the corporate engines to create untold wealth. Let the natural market forces play without political interference. And politicians, they assure us, are surely not to be trusted. What the elite really mean is that democracy is not to be trusted. [Journalist] Lewis Lapham wrote of the modern global capitalists he met at the World Economic Forum in Davos, Switzerland, in the spring of 1998:

> Having achieved their success by virtue of their talent for organization, they defined the dilemma of postmodern capitalism as a problem in management rather than a question of politics. Politicians were by definition untrustworthy, belonging to one of only two familiar types—light-minded demagogues stirring up crowds, or "pesky legislators" constantly bothering people with demands for bribes. Markets might have their flaws, but government was worse. Political interference wrecked the free play of natural distribution, and government never knew how to manage anything—not roads, not dairy farms or gambling casinos or capital flows. All would be well, and civilization much improved, if only politics could be manufactured in the way that one manufactured railroad cars or tomato soup.

A belief in the conscience of the market, with no checks by government or an economic power like labor, will spell disaster for democracy. A market economy without restraint—with no environmental or food safety rules, with no labor rights, with no labor unions—will undermine democratic institutions as all power accrues to a corporate elite. "If labor has no role," [labor union] AFL-CIO president John Sweeney told the largely unsympathetic crowd at the World Economic Forum in Davos, "democracy has no future."

Periodical Bibliography

The following articles have been selected to supplement the diverse views presented in this chapter.

Grant Aldonas — "Has the North American Free Trade Agreement Been a Success?" *International Debates*, May 2005.

John A. Baden — "The Pathological Politics of Trade," Foundation for Research on Economics and the Environment, March 17, 2004. www.free-eco.org.

John W. Foster — "NAFTA at Ten: Nothing to Celebrate," *Canadian Dimension*, March-April 2004.

James K. Galbraith — "What Kind of Economy?" *Nation*, March 5, 2007.

Erika Kinetz — "Trading Down," *Harper's Magazine*, 2005.

Frank LaGrotta — "'Outsourcing' Our Lives," *Nation*, March 8, 2004.

New Republic — "Unfair," July 7, 2004.

Eric Pape et al. — "Rising Barriers," *Newsweek*, March 20, 2006.

William Poole — "A Perspective on U.S. International Trade," *Federal Reserve Bank of Saint Louis Review*, March-April 2004.

Sheridan Prasso — "Trading Up," *New Republic*, August 16, 2004.

Sherle R. Schwenninger — "A Goldilocks World Economy?" *World Policy Journal*, Winter 2006.

E. Timothy Smith — "From Miami to Quebec and Beyond: Opposition to the Free Trade Area of the Americas," *Peace & Change*, April 2004.

Lawrence H. Summers — "America Overdrawn," *Foreign Policy*, July-August 2004.

CHAPTER 2

Does Free Trade Help the Developing World?

Chapter Preface

Some see free trade as the most effective way to aid people in poorer parts of the world, while others point to continuing poverty in developing countries that have adopted free trade. At times the pro-free-traders seem to have the upper hand, being able to point to success stories, but expert opinion has gone back and forth on the issue for over a century.

In the nineteenth century, many Latin American nations pursued export-oriented policies; countries such as Argentina and Brazil stressed export of agricultural commodities. This left these countries vulnerable to declines in the world price for products such as beef, sugar, or coffee. Moreover, agriculture did not provide many high-paying jobs that could absorb burgeoning populations. In the 1950s and 1960s many countries attempted to improve their economies by "import-substitution industrialization," instituting high tariffs on imported manufactured items in an attempt to establish domestic production of goods such as automobiles, household appliances, and electronics. These policies had mixed results at best, as University of California, Berkeley economist J. Bradford DeLong has written: "Too much of import-substitution industrialization—Argentina's attempt to build an auto industry, Brazil's attempt to build a minicomputer industry—had its principal effect in reducing the real incomes of individuals and the efficiency of firms that had to buy from local producers."

Advocates of free trade believe the high-tariff, import-substitution approach was fundamentally wrong. They point to success stories such as Taiwan and Singapore as examples of nations that have prospered because of free trade. The former British colony of Hong Kong, for example, had a very nearly perfect free-trade policy. The city-state was a favorite example of the late Nobel laureate in economics Milton Friedman. He wrote that facing an increasing population with few natural resources, "the salvation of Hong Kong has been its completely free trade and free market policy. No tariffs on imports, no subsidies or other privileges to exports." According to Friedman this policy led to a dramatic increase in living standards, despite the colony's resources being strained by a large influx of refugees from Communist China.

However, some experts are skeptical of the Asian success stories. The skeptics believe that the Asian model—excluding British-governed Hong Kong—is less about free trade and more about restricting imports while producing as much as possible for export. For example, a report published by MCB Bank of Pakistan notes that the Asian model of growth through trade has "facilitated the export-oriented growth of the [Chinese and] other Asian economies . . . by accommodating to mercantilist, export-oriented Asian economic models. Subsequently these economies recorded huge trade surpluses while the overall trade balance for the U.S. deteriorated." With a weakening dollar and ever-increasing trade balances, the clamor in Congress for trade barriers will grow, a move that could leave many developing countries with a reduced opportunity to export goods to the United States. Even if trade barriers are not increased, America's ability to buy goods from abroad will likely decrease, leaving countries that focused on export-oriented development struggling to find a market.

Other developments in Asia, Africa, and Latin America have also called into question the benefits of free trade. The emphasis on trade liberalization in the 1990s has meant increasing competition among poor countries. The Federal Reserve Bank has reported that during the early 2000s Mexico lost over 20 percent of the jobs in its assembly (or *maquiladora*) plants—factories that produced for the U.S. market. These losses were a result of competition from China and other developing countries that entered the market. Meanwhile small farmers in the less-developed world are being hurt by competition from multinational corporations. "Competitive pressures induced by trade liberalization [in the mid-1990s] led to the expansion of commercial plantations at the expense of smallholders," according to Walden Bello, a professor of sociology and director of the think tank Focus on the Global South.

Such negative developments call into question the benefits of free trade for the developing world, but economists and others devoted to free trade maintain that they are a natural part of adjustments in a liberalized economy; while some people lose, they say, most citizens of poorer countries benefit from free trade. The following chapter explores these issues.

> *"Freer trade is associated with higher growth and that higher growth is associated with reduced poverty."*

Free Trade Has Reduced Poverty in the Developing World

Jagdish Bhagwati

Jagdish Bhagwati is a well-known economist from India who has specialized in free-trade and development issues. He is the author of In Defense of Globalization, *from which this viewpoint is taken, and of numerous academic articles. Bhagwati makes the case that export-oriented free trade promotes growth and that growth in turn reduces poverty. He presents historical evidence, both case studies and statistical studies that economists call regressions, showing that in most instances countries with "outward-looking" trade-oriented economies have grown at a rapid rate. In contrast, what Bhagwati calls "autarkic" economies, in which policy makers aim for self-sufficiency, have lagged behind in both growth and poverty reduction.*

As you read, consider the following questions:

1. Which countries, when added to the analysis of nineteenth-century economic growth, proved crucial in showing that free-trade was beneficial to national economies, according to the author?
2. In Bhagwati's view, how did India's economic experience from the 1960s to the 1980s differ from that of countries of the Far East such as Korea and Taiwan?
3. In addition to economic policies, what factor does the author cite as important in helping countries of the Far East grow their economies?

[I]s optimism about the benign relationship between trade and growth . . . justified despite the fact that one could readily imagine circumstances where, instead of helping growth, trade could harm or even bypass growth? Indeed, economists can, and do, readily build formal models to derive these unpleasant possibilities. We need, however, to know *empirically* what happens in practice. And empirical evidence supports the optimism.

Evidence of Trade Benefits

First, consider the late nineteenth century. Historians of this period have often thought that protection, not free trade, was associated with high growth. Paul Bairoch, in the *Cambridge Economic History of Europe*, has argued that "protectionism [went with] economic growth and expansion of trade; liberalism [went with] stagnation in both." Recently, the economic historians Kevin O'Rourke and Jeff Williamson have reinforced this impression by deriving a statistical association, through running what statisticians call regressions, between economic growth and import tariffs from 1875 to 1914.

But the later work of [economist] Douglas Irwin has refuted that proposition. By adding to the regression analysis several countries that were on the periphery of the world economy but integrating into it, as one should, Irwin manages to break the positive association between tariffs and growth. Equally important, he shows that the rapidly growing countries Canada and Argentina had high tariffs but that these tariffs were for revenue and had few protective side effects. The two countries were in fact splendid examples of outward-oriented countries that built prosperity on their pro-trade orientation.

Analyses of Specific Industries

Second, we can also turn to analyses that take into account complexities that the many-country regressions necessarily ignore. These typically involve deeper examination of specific episodes that speak to the issue at hand or consist of sophisticated country studies in depth.

Two examples of such analyses, both supportive of the merits of freer trade, can be found in the empirical literature. Just because specific tariffs led an industry to grow, we cannot conclude that the strategy contributed to economic prosperity and hence growth. Recognizing this, Irwin has produced a fascinating case study of whether a classic "infant industry" tariff levied in the late nineteenth century in the United States on the tinplate industry really promoted that industry *and* whether that promotion was cost-effective. Irwin's careful answer is that the [President William] McKinley tariff protection accelerated the establishment of the industry by a mere ten years, since the U.S. prices of iron and steel inputs were already converging with those in Britain and therefore making U.S. production of tinplate profitable in any event, but that this acceleration was economically expensive because it does not pass a cost-benefit test.

Reasons for Export-Oriented Success

At the same time, the modern evidence against an inward-looking or import substitution trade strategy is really quite overwhelming. In the 1960s and 1970s, several full-length

Denouncing Globalization Is Risky

All the ritualistic denunciations of globalization are not harmless. Psychology matters. If global investors fear that the United States might make its economy less open to foreign trade and investment, the result might be the very dollar panic that everyone fears. The dollar's status as the world's central international currency depends on its usefulness in buying and selling. The more we restrict, the less useful it becomes. Globalization's casual bashers should remember that. They think they're playing only to a domestic audience, but the world is listening, and it may not like what it hears.

Robert J. Samuelson, Washington Post, *October 24, 2007.*

studies of the trade and industrialization strategies of over a dozen major developing countries, including India, Ghana, Egypt, South Korea, the Philippines, Chile, Brazil, and Mexico, were undertaken at the Organization for Economic Cooperation and Development (OECD) and the National Bureau of Economic Research, the leading research institution in the United States. These studies were very substantial and examined several complexities that would be ignored in a simplistic regression analysis across a multitude of nations. Thus, for instance, in examining whether the 1966 trade liberalization in India worked, [Indian economist] T.N. Srinivasan and I wrote a whole chapter assessing whether, after making allowance for a severe drought that blighted exports, the liberalization could be considered to have been beneficial compared to a decision to avoid it. Only after systematic examination of the actual details of these countries' experience could we judge whether trade liberalization had truly occurred and when; only then we could shift meaningfully to a limited regression analysis that stood on the shoulders of this sophisticated analysis. The result was to overturn decisively the prevailing wisdom in favor of autarkic policies. Indeed, many of us had started with the presumption that inward-looking policies would be seen to be welfare-enhancing, but the results were strikingly in the opposite direction, supportive of outward orientation in trade and direct foreign investment instead. Why?

- The outward-oriented economies were better able to gain from trade. The layman finds it hard to appreciate this because, as the Nobel laureate Paul Samuelson has remarked, perhaps the most counterintuitive but true proposition in economics has to be that one can specialize and do better.

- Economists today also appreciate that there are scale economies in production that can be exploited when trade expands markets. This is particularly the case for small countries. For this reason, Tanzania, Uganda, and Kenya, which had protected themselves with high tariffs against imports in the 1960s, found that the cost of their protection was excessively high, with each country producing a few units of several items. They decided in the 1970s therefore to have an East African Common Market so that they could specialize among themselves and each could produce at lower cost for the larger combined market.

- Then there are the gains from increased competition. Restriction of trade often is the chief cause of domestic monopolies. Freer trade produces enhanced competition and gains therefrom. India provides an amusing illustration. Sheltered from import competition, Indian car manufacturers produced such shoddy cars that, when they went up to India's Tariff Commission for renewal of their protection, the commissioners wryly remarked that in Indian cars, everything made a noise except the horn!

- In order to maintain outward orientation, countries must create macroeconomic stability (chiefly, low inflation). Inflation-prone economies with fixed exchange rate regimes, where countries only reluctantly adjust their exchange rates in response to inflation, would soon find that their currency had become overvalued. This overvaluation would make exporting less profitable and importing more rewarding, thus undermining the outward-oriented trade strategy. Hence countries committed to [an] export-promoting trade strategy had to have macroeconomic stability, and they therefore earned the economic advantages that follow from good management of the economy. . . .

- Finally . . . , direct foreign investment would also be lower in the presence of trade restrictions. It would also be less productive. Trade barriers would mean that such investment would have to be primarily for the domestic market, which was generally limited, whereas in outward-oriented economies it would be for world markets, which were not. Then again, just as trade barriers reduce the efficiency of domestic investments and incur the loss from protection, so do they reduce the efficiency of foreign investments.

Export-Oriented Growth in East Asia

Third, consider the contrasting experience of India and the Far East. From the 1960s to the 1980s, India remained locked in relatively autarkic trade policies; the Far Eastern countries—Singapore, Hong Kong, South Korea, and Taiwan, the four Little Tigers—shifted to outward orientation dramatically. The results speak for themselves: exports and income grew at abysmal rates in India, at dramatic rates in the Far East. India missed the bus. No, it missed the Concorde! . . .

The high rates of investment reflected, in turn, the fact that the East Asian countries turned outward beginning in the 1960s and therefore had world markets to work with when planning their investments. By contrast, India turned inward, so its investment was constrained by the growth of the domestic market. Growth in that market in a largely agricultural country meant the growth of agricultural output and incomes. But nowhere in the world has agriculture grown, on a sustained basis, at more than 4 percent annually, making it a weak basis for a strong investment performance!

The Far East's phenomenally high investment rates also were exceptionally productive. They were based on export earnings, which therefore enabled the investment to occur with imported capital equipment embodying advanced and productive technology. Besides, these countries had inherited tremendously high literacy rates that ensured the productive use of new technologies. Accommodating, even ahead-of-the-curve expansion of higher education also helped to increase the productivity of the investment. So the Far East generally was characterized by a virtuous interaction among beneficial policies: outward orientation, high literacy, and emphasis on higher education. . . .

Trade Boosts Growth

Fourth, what do the many multi-country cross-sectional studies of this question show today? Not all show a positive relationship between trade and growth. What one can say, however, is that such statistical evidence, by and large, is consonant with the views of the free trade proponents.

The latest set of such studies, by David Dollar and Aart Kraay of the World Bank, show that if one focuses on post-1980 globalizers such as Vietnam and Mexico, which were in the top third of developing countries in terms of the increase in the share of trade in GDP [gross domestic product] during 1977–1997, they show better growth performance. Since trade will generally grow even if trade barriers are not reduced, it is important to note that this group also cut import tariffs by three times as much as the non-globalizing two-thirds. These authors also observe that while growth rates in the non-globalizing developing countries have generally slowed down in the past two decades, globalizers have shown exactly the opposite pattern, with their growth rates accelerating from the level of the 1960s and 1970s. This is certainly true for China, and to a lesser but certain degree for India, two countries that together have nearly 2.5 billion people within their borders.

So, with the usual caveat that in the social sciences one can rarely establish the degree of credibility for one's argument that one can aspire to in the physical sciences, one can conclude that freer trade is associated with higher growth and that higher growth is associated with reduced poverty. Hence, growth reduces poverty.

> *"Free trade policies that once promised an influx of export-related jobs now serve as an open door through which the manufacturing base can drain away to lower-wage locales."*

Free Trade Has Hurt Some Economies in the Developing World

Gordon Lafer

In the following viewpoint, Gordon Lafer makes the case that poorer countries are hurt by a blind devotion to free trade. He uses the example of an employee-owned bicycle manufacturing company in Mexico to demonstrate the negative impact of free-trade agreements. NAFTA (North American Free Trade Agreement), the 1994 treaty with Mexico, the United States, and Canada, led to competition in Mexico from bicycle tires made in China and shipped through the United States to avoid Mexican tariffs. This competition eventually forced the Mexican business to close. Gordon Lafer is an associate professor at the University of Oregon's Labor Education and Research Center. He has also taught at the Universidad Latina de América in Morelia, Mexico.

Gordon Lafer, "The Last Bicycle Tire Plant," *Dissent*, Summer 2005, pp. 5–8. Copyright © 2005 by Dissent Publishing Corporation. Reproduced by permission.

As you read, consider the following questions:

1. How many jobs in Mexico's manufacturing sector have been lost since its employment peak, according to the author?
2. According to Lafer, what is the principal reason that bicycle tires from China are less expensive than Mexican-made ones?
3. To which sector of the economy are both Mexicans and Americans turning in order to avoid Chinese competition, in the author's opinion?

When Americans think about free trade and Mexico, we usually think of one thing: the giant sucking sound of U.S. jobs being lost to cheaper labor in the south. We lose, they gain. Our family-wage jobs become their $2 per hour step up from rural poverty; that's the shorthand summary of what the North American Free Trade Agreement (NAFTA) looks like from our side of the border.

Mexican Workers Are Too Expensive

If that story was true at one point, however, it is no longer. Barely ten years since NAFTA was signed, many Mexicans find themselves in a position surprisingly similar to that of American workers: apparently too expensive for international investors, they're watching their jobs leave the country by the tens of thousands.

For the past twenty years, Mexico has been the premier model of neoliberal reform. The size of government has been reduced and public enterprises privatized; social benefits of all kinds have been slashed, and the country has been opened up to foreign investment with few if any restrictions. For two decades, the national economic strategy has boiled down to one thought: make the country more attractive to foreign investors. Indeed, Mexico has signed more free trade agreements than any other country in the world.

During this period, successive presidents have promised the populace that temporary sacrifice would lead to long-term prosperity. For a number of years following the adoption of NAFTA, the country indeed became a magnet for foreign capital, and employment in export-producing *maquiladoras* grew rapidly.[1] Only ten years after signing that treaty, however, the country's fortunes have reversed. Despite every effort to attract foreign capital with low wages and little regulation, Mexico now finds itself overpriced in the world market. Even in the *maquiladora* factories of the border zone, Mexican workers make $1.50–$2.00 per hour—significantly above the Chinese minimum of 25 cents per hour. The same free trade policies that once promised an influx of export-related jobs now serve as an open door through which the manufacturing base can drain away to lower-wage locales.

Since peaking in the late 1990s, Mexico has lost more than five hundred thousand manufacturing jobs—above all to China. Moreover, the impact of free trade is not limited to the export sector. Even locally owned factories producing for the domestic market have come under increasing pressure from a rising tide of east Asian imports produced at costs that no Mexican firm can match.

An Innovative Local Business

One example of the difficulties facing even the most innovative of Mexican enterprises is the Trademh cooperative, which in 2002 became the last bicycle tire producer in the country. If one were looking for a textbook example of local economic development, the Trademh story might serve as a best-case model of how to do things right. International development experts frequently hail the importance of small-scale loans and "micro enterprise" development. Indeed, these strategies are specifically promoted as a more stable alternative to

1. Maquiladoras are factories, typically located close to the U.S.–Mexico border, which specialize in assembly of finished consumer products from parts manufactured elsewhere.

export-based growth. By cultivating smaller enterprises focused on local needs, the argument goes, poorer nations can build up internal markets while strengthening local communities. This cooperative was a perfect example of such a strategy.

Trademh's origins date from an early-1990s labor struggle at Tornel, a large tire manufacturer in Mexico City. Tornel's employees sought to democratize their union, specifically demanding the right to elect their own leadership and to force Tornel to respect national wage standards. Officially, the employees were represented by a government-affiliated union. But the union "leaders," who were openly paid by the company, understood their jobs as guaranteeing labor peace for the company and union votes for the ruling party. Over a period of years, employee activists were threatened, beaten, and kidnapped; police-escorted thugs attacked workers when they tried to cast ballots for an independent union; and numerous appeals to government officials were rejected. Ultimately, Tornel laid off six hundred employees in a mass firing that crushed the independent union movement.

Workers Become Entrepreneurs

At this point in the story, one might assume that the protagonists, defeated and exhausted, would give up. Instead, the Tornel employees took their mass layoff as the starting point for an even more ambitious project. Mexican law requires severance pay for fired employees, and Tornel complied with this aspect of the law. Of the 600 employees who were fired for union activity, 125 decided to pool their severance pay in order to form a cooperative enterprise that would produce bicycle tires.

Naming their cooperative Trademh (a Spanish acronym for Democratic Rubber Workers) the 125 members set out to teach themselves how to be entrepreneurs. They canvassed a variety of state and local governments before deciding to settle in Morelia, the capital of the state of Michoacán, about four hours outside Mexico City. They worked at securing financing, obtaining an appropriate site, and teaching themselves how to run a business. In October 1994, with partial financing from a local agency, they ordered the necessary equipment from a European supplier. Their commitment was quickly put to the test two months later when the peso was devalued by half, doubling the effective purchase price overnight. The members gathered together and voted to take on increased personal debt in order to buy the machinery, gambling that their venture would ultimately be profitable enough to pay off the added expense.

During the course of a year, the co-op members themselves did all the construction work necessary to build their factory. In 1995, Trademh produced its first tire, and the business grew quickly. The company produced half a million tires in 1996 and nearly one million in 1997. When they began, the workers set a goal of producing a hundred thousand tires per month; by 1998 they had reached and surpassed this milestone. The factory workers, who started off sleeping in bunk beds off the factory floor, were now able to get mortgages and bring their families from Mexico City to move into new houses.

A Doomed Social Experiment

At the same time, the cooperative dedicated itself to a "social project" in addition to the "economic project" of the factory. The first goal of this project was to improve the education level of the co-op members themselves. After constructing the factory, the cooperative built a two-room schoolhouse and cultural center on the adjacent lot. The cooperative operated on strict democratic principles, and early in its existence the members voted to require all workers to take classes after their shifts were done. Within five years, forty members of the cooperative had completed elementary school, and another forty completed junior high school. In addition, Trademh became a

Chinese Wages Far Below Mexican Wages

Chinese workers remain among the lowest paid in the world. The average total labor compensation for a Chinese manufacturing worker is 57 cents per hour, with many making far less than that, benefits included.

An average Chinese wage of $0.57 per hour—or $104 per month—is about 3 percent of the average U.S. manufacturing worker's wage, according to data collected by [demographer Judith] Banister. "Equally as striking, regional competitors in the newly industrialized economies of Asia had, on average, manufacturing labor costs more than 10 times those for China's manufacturing workers, and Mexico and Brazil had manufacturing labor costs about four times those for China's manufacturing employees."

Richard McCormack,
Manufacturing and Technology News,
May 2, 2006.

central force in the surrounding community—sponsoring a sports league, providing construction materials for area schools, and offering free adult education classes open to any member of the community.

But the co-op was living on borrowed time. The seeds of Trademh's destruction had been sown in 1994 with the signing of NAFTA. The Trademh workers were doomed from the day they started; they just didn't realize it until it was too late.

Competition from China

Based on past trends, Trademh expected to sell 1.4 million tires in the year 2000, marking a nearly 30 percent annual growth rate. Instead, the co-op found its sales inexplicably declining and set out to discover why. As members began questioning customers, the workers discovered a disturbing answer: millions of bicycle tires were being imported from East Asia at prices that no Mexican manufacturer could match. In some cases, they found tires imported as contraband—arriving in a ship container marked as another good but stuffed with tires. In other cases, the deception was more sophisticated, and specifically facilitated by NAFTA. Trademh activists reported finding tires being sold with a "Made in the USA" stamp in 1997—ten years after the last American bicycle tire factory closed down. In some cases, careful examination showed a "Produced in China" mark inside the seam of the tire. Because NAFTA had eliminated import tariffs against U.S.—but not Chinese—products, Chinese producers could evade Mexican taxes by shipping products first to the United States and then importing them, duty-free, into Mexico. This practice was not legal, but neither was it policed. The import of cheap Asian tires quickly swamped the market. In 1995, the value of bicycle tires imported to Mexico stood at $6 million; by 2002 it had more than tripled, to nearly $20 million.

Trademh cut all possible costs in order to lower its selling price. Ultimately, the co-op reduced its cost of production to 23 pesos (approximately $2 US) per tire. By contrast, Asian tires were coming into the country at a cost of 14 pesos apiece. At this rate, every bicycle tire manufacturer in Mexico would soon be out of business.

The price difference between Asian and domestic tires was all the more striking given the fixed costs of tire production. The single most important input—rubber—is priced on an international commodity market and therefore costs the same no matter where tires are made. The machinery of production is likewise internationally traded and therefore provides little price advantage to one locale or another. Virtually the entire price difference is due to labor costs. Trademh's members were up against the simple, brutal fact that poorer or more desperate workers elsewhere were willing to work for less. . . .

The End of an Industry

In 2002, Trademh turned off its machines and closed its doors, marking the end of a heroic—and briefly triumphant—effort to carve out a dignified life for this group of manufacturing workers.

When Trademh shut down, it was the last bicycle tire manufacturer in the country. Mexicans buy nearly twenty million bicycle tires per year. As recently as 1998, most of this market was supplied by four domestic manufacturers. By 2001, three of the four had closed; Trademh remained in business so long because it had an unusually strong interest in protecting the jobs of its members. But no matter how it trimmed costs, it could not compete with cheaper imports. In January 2002, the National Association of Bicycle Manufacturers canceled its contract with Trademh, noting that the price difference between domestic and imported tires was too great for it to continue buying locally. Shortly thereafter, the company surrendered to the reality of international market forces.

Today, the Trademh factory stands as a testament to the ravages of free trade policy. When the cooperative went bankrupt, the federal government seized its factory in lieu of unpaid back taxes. However, the machines can't be sold to any Mexican company—because no one can afford to produce bicycle tires domestically—and the government has not yet taken the steps needed to find a foreign buyer. Three years later, all the machines stand silently in place. "It's so frustrating to see the machinery here, to want to work and not to be able to do anything," says Soto Romero. The on-site classrooms likewise remain unaltered—books on the shelves, chairs at the ready, but no one allowed to use the space. It's heartbreaking to visit the Trademh site—to see the results of a bold project, standing just as they were and still ready to be used.

It's tempting to think that, if the government would just re-lease its hold on the site, the workers could again be back at the machines and the community alive with education. But the death of Trademh is determined by something far more implacable than the whim of government officials. Even the most sympathetic official could not undo the terms of Mexico's commitments to the International Monetary Fund, the World Trade Organization, or NAFTA. It is these, far more than the indifference of bureaucrats, that keeps Trademh's ma-chines idled.

Indeed, in the fall of 2004 Mexico established new trade terms with China, which lifted import duties on Chinese-made tires. Thus, while Trademh activists spent countless meetings trying to get government officials to take responsi-bility for illegal imports destroying local manufacturing, the government found a completely opposite solution to this prob-lem: it legalized the imports. Now, this is no longer a problem of law, and there is no need for Chinese imports to be trans-shipped through the United States. But the result for Mexican workers is the same.

Turning to the Service Sector

For a brief period, Trademh stood as a shining example of how determined workers could construct a new and dignified life for themselves, their families, and the surrounding com-munity. "We were really scratching glory for a while there," says Soto Romero. The co-op's destruction has been predict-ably traumatic for its members. Most have drifted away—back to Mexico City or wherever they can find work. Many have been unable to find work of any kind.

Recently, fifteen of Trademh's remaining members formed a new cooperative—this time aimed at providing building and machinery maintenance and repair services for local offices. Once again, the co-op members have committed themselves to goals of self- and community improvement beyond their own financial well-being. It is telling that they have been driven out of manufacturing and into the service economy, mirroring the experience of millions of Americans. Here in the rich north, local governments, labor unions, and individual families have largely reacted to globalization by turning away from manufacturing and concentrating on work in the profitable parts of the service industry. It is not clear that this strategy can work to sustain the millions of Americans in need of family-wage jobs. For Mexico, with a much smaller commercial service industry and much greater need, the prospects are yet more daunting.

> *"Deep cuts in subsidies and trade barriers would save U.S. taxpayers and consumers tens of billions of dollars. . . while potentially opening markets abroad."*

Trade Barriers Hurt American Consumers and Developing-World Farmers

Daniel Griswold, Stephen Slivinski, and Christopher Preble

Daniel Griswold is director of the Center for Trade Policy Studies at the CATO Institute, a libertarian think tank; Stephen Slivinski is the center's director of budget studies, and Christopher Preble is director of foreign policy studies. In the following viewpoint, the authors make the case that subsidies to farmers in the United States, both in the form of direct payment to farmers and higher prices due to tariffs on agricultural goods, hurt developing-world farmers and American consumers. The authors believe that tariff reduction would benefit everyone except a few large argribusinesses.

Daniel Griswold, Stephen Slivinski, and Christopher Preble, "6 Reasons to Kill Farm Subsidies and Trade Barriers," *Reason*, vol. 37, February 2006. Copyright © 2006 by Reason Foundation, 3415 S. Sepulveda Blvd., Suite 400, Los Angeles, CA 90034, www.reason.com. Reproduced by permission.

As you read, consider the following questions:

1. How much do farm subsidies and tariffs (the "food tax") cost the average American household per year, according to the authors?

2. By how much would a one-third reduction in tariffs increase global production and American production, in Griswold, Slivinski, and Preble's view?

3. According to the authors, why would a reduction in trade barriers for agricultural products benefit the United States' position in international affairs?

America's agricultural policies have remained fundamentally unchanged for nearly three-quarters of a century. The U.S. government continues to subsidize the production of rice, milk, sugar, cotton, peanuts, tobacco, and other commodities, while restricting imports to maintain artificially high domestic prices. The competition and innovation that have changed the face of the planet have been effectively locked out of America's farm economy by politicians who fear farm voters more than the dispersed consumers who subsidize them. . . .

Lower Food Prices for Americans

The foremost reason to curtail farm protectionism is to benefit American consumers. By shielding the domestic market from global competition, government farm programs raise the cost of food and with it the overall cost of living. According to the Organization for Economic Cooperation and Development, the higher domestic food prices caused by U.S. farm programs transferred $16.2 billion from American consumers to domestic agricultural producers in 2004. That amounts to an annual "food tax" per household of $146. This consumer tax is paid over and above what we dole out to farmers through the federal budget.

American consumers pay more than double the world price for sugar. The federal sugar program guarantees domestic producers a take of 22.9 cents per pound for beet sugar and 18 cents for cane sugar, while the world spot price for raw cane sugar is currently about 10 cents per pound. A 2000 study by the General Accounting Office estimated that Americans paid an extra $1.9 billion a year for sugar due to import quotas alone.

American families also pay more for their milk, butter, and cheese, thanks to federal dairy price supports and trade barriers. The federal government administers a byzantine system of domestic price supports, marketing orders, import controls, export subsidies, and domestic and international giveaway programs. According to the U.S. International Trade Commission, between 2000 and 2002 the average domestic price of nonfat dry milk was 23 percent higher than the world price, cheese 37 percent higher, and butter more than double. Trade policies also drive up prices for peanuts, cotton, beef, orange juice, canned tuna, and other products.

These costs are compounded by escalating tariffs based on the amount of processing embodied in a product. If the government allowed lower, market prices for commodity inputs, processed foods would be substantially cheaper. Lifting sugar protection, for example, would apply downward pressure on the prices we pay for candy, soft drinks, bakery goods, and other sugar-containing products.

The burden of higher domestic food costs falls disproportionately on poor households. Farm protections act as a regressive tax, with higher prices at the grocery store negating some or all of the income support the government seeks to deliver via programs such as food stamps.

If American farm subsidies and trade barriers were significantly reduced, millions of American households would enjoy higher real incomes.

Benefits of Farm Reform

Producers who export goods to the rest of the world and manufacturers who use agricultural inputs would also stand to benefit significantly from farm reform. So would their employees.

When government intervention raises domestic prices for raw materials and other commodities, it imposes higher costs on "downstream" users in the supply chain. Those higher costs can mean higher prices for consumers, reduced global competitiveness for American exporters, lower sales, less investment, and ultimately fewer employment opportunities and lower pay in the affected industries. Artificially high commodity prices drive domestic producers abroad to seek cheaper inputs—or out of business altogether.

In the last two decades, the number of sugar refineries in the U.S. has dwindled from 23 to eight, largely because of the doubled price of domestic raw sugar. During the last decade thousands of jobs have been lost in the confectionary industry, with losses especially heavy in the Chicago area. Expensive food also hurts restaurants.

Enterprises outside the food business would benefit from farm reform as well. Rich countries' agricultural trade barriers remain the single greatest obstacle to a comprehensive World Trade Organization (WTO) agreement on trade liberalization. . . .

A 2001 study by Drusilla Brown at Tufts University and Alan Deardorff and Robert Stern at the University of Michigan estimated that even a one-third cut in tariffs on agriculture, industry, and services would boost annual global production by $613 billion, including $177 billion in the United States—or about $1,700 per American household. Some of the country's most competitive sectors, including information technology, financial services, insurance, and consulting, probably would increase their share of global markets if the Doha Round were successful.[1] Farm reform remains the key.

A common argument against liberalization is that the U.S. should hold onto its agricultural tariffs as "bargaining chips" in WTO negotiations. The worry is that if we were to dismantle our barriers unilaterally, other countries would lose any incentive to give up theirs.

But reducing *protectionism* would not primarily be a "concession" to other countries. It would be a favor to ourselves. In the process we would set a good example and create good will in global negotiations, inviting other countries to join us in realizing the benefits of lower domestic food costs. . . .

A More Hospitable World

The collective effect of American farm policies is to depress the income of agricultural producers worldwide, exacerbating poverty in areas, such as sub-Saharan Africa and Central Asia, where people are heavily dependent on agriculture.

The frustration and despair caused by these policies undermine American security. Many people who depend on agriculture for their survival, both as a source of nourishment and a means of acquiring wealth, perceive U.S. farm policy as part of an anti-American narrative in which Washington wants to keep the rest of the world locked in poverty. Indeed, in a survey of anti-American sentiment around the world, the Pew Research Center found a majority of respondents in more than a dozen countries were convinced that U.S. farm and trade policies increased the "poverty gap" worldwide. These sentiments transcended geographic, ethnic, or religious boundaries. In such an environment, terrorist ringleaders find fertile ground for their message of hate and violence.

Nicholas Stern, chief economist at the World Bank, is blunt about America's leadership role. "It is hypocritical to preach

1. The Doha round of trade talks was held by the World Trade Organization starting in November 2001 in Doha, Qatar. They were stalled as of spring 2008.

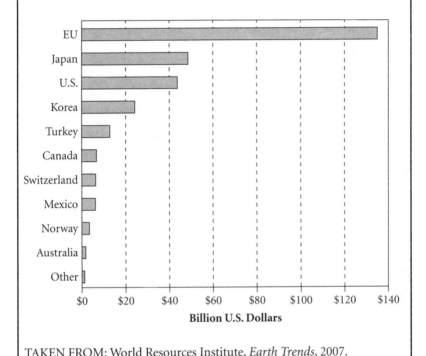

Agricultural Subsidies, 2005

Between 1993 and 2006, the U.S. annual trade deficit—the value of goods and services exported minus the value of goods and services imported—increased almost ten-fold.

TAKEN FROM: World Resources Institute, *Earth Trends*, 2007.

the advantages of free trade and free markets," Stern told the U.N. publication *Africa Recovery*, "and then erect obstacles in precisely those markets in which developing countries have a comparative advantage." Johan Norberg, of the Swedish think tank Timbro, argues that farm protection in developed countries amounts to a "deliberate and systematic means of undermining the very type of industry in which the developing countries do have comparative advantages."

American subsidies and tariffs amount to much more money than its foreign aid to the developing world. According to Oxfam, "in crop year 2002, the U.S. government provided

$3.4 billion in total subsidies to the cotton sector," including about 25,000 growers. "To put this figure into perspective," Oxfam says, "it is nearly twice the total amount of U.S. foreign aid given to sub-Saharan Africa. It is also more than the GDP [gross domestic product] of Benin, Burkina Faso, or Chad, the main cotton-producing countries in the region." The subsidies drive down world cotton prices, costing developing countries billions of dollars in lost export earnings.

Real Reform Would Benefit Everyone

Poor countries don't want our pity; they want our respect. To the extent that American security depends on the expansion of liberal democratic institutions and free market economics, Washington must be particularly sensitive to policies that exacerbate poverty in the developing world. . . .

A farm bill with deep cuts in subsidies and trade barriers would save U.S. taxpayers and consumers tens of billions of dollars during the next decade while potentially opening markets abroad for tens of billions more in American exports across the economy. Congress and the president should seize the opportunity to bring America's farm sector into the nurturing sunlight of an open global market.

"*Mexico should have reaped the rewards of [trade] liberalization. It hasn't.*"

NAFTA Has Hurt Mexico's Farmers and Workers

Timothy A. Wise

Timothy A. Wise is deputy director of the Global Development and Environment Institute at Tufts University. He coauthored A Survey of Sustainable Development: Social and Economic Dimensions *and has written extensively on free trade's impact on rural communities in the developing world.*

In the following viewpoint, written ten years after the North American Free Trade Agreement (NAFTA) signing, Wise appraises the effect free trade has had on rural Mexico. He contends that instead of bringing development to Mexican agriculture, NAFTA has forced thousands of small farmers to give up growing crops. Poverty has increased, and many Mexican peasants have been compelled to seek work in the cities or in the United States, Wise maintains.

As you read, consider the following questions:

1. What are two indications that Mexico has become more involved in world trade since 1985, according to Wise?

Timothy A. Wise, "NAFTA's Untold Stories: Mexico's Grassroots Responses to North American Integration," *America's Program Policy Report*, June 2003. www.americas policy.org. Reproduced by permission of the author.

2. What are some of the reasons Mexican coffee producers
   and grain farmers have become poorer, in the author's
   view?

3. According to Wise, what does the Mexican government
   need to do in order to balance out the harsh effects of
   free trade?

Although some policymakers still point to Mexico as a success story, there is a growing consensus that the free trade
experiment has not lived up to expectations. This has important implications for a host of new trade agreements now under consideration [in 2003]. Most important are the World
Trade Organization's Doha Round and the Free Trade Area of
the Americas (FTAA), but agreements are being finalized with
Central America, Chile, and other nations. Like the FTAA,
which the [George W.] Bush administration has presented as a
"NAFTA for the hemisphere," most reflect the trade and investment rules established by the North American agreement.

NAFTA's Poor Record

NAFTA is no model for sustainable development despite its
success in transforming one of the world's most protected
economies into one of its most open. Since 1985, when Mexico
began its rapid liberalization process, exports have doubled
and foreign direct investment has nearly tripled. According to
the NAFTA model, with inflation significantly in check, Mexico
should have reaped the rewards of liberalization. It hasn't.

According to official figures [as of 2003] from the World
Bank and the Mexican government:

- Economic growth has been slow. Since 1985, Mexico
  has seen per capita real growth of just 1%, compared
  to 3.4% from 1960 to 1980.

- Job growth has been sluggish. There has been little job
  creation, falling far short of the demand in Mexico

from new entrants into the labor force. Manufacturing, one of the few sectors to show significant economic growth, has seen a net loss in jobs since NAFTA took effect. This is despite a 45% increase in productivity.

- The new jobs are not good jobs. Some 60% of the employed do not receive any of the benefits mandated by Mexican law. One-third of the economically active population works in the informal sector.

- Wages have declined. The real minimum wage is down 60% since 1982, 23% under NAFTA. Contractual wages are down 55% since 1987. Manufacturing wages are down 12% under NAFTA.

- Poverty has increased. The number of households living in poverty has grown 80% since 1984, with some 75% of Mexico's people now below the poverty line. Income distribution has become more lopsided, leaving Mexico with one of the hemisphere's worst records.

- The rural sector is in crisis, beset by grain imports from the United States, decreasing commodity prices, and reduced government support. Four-fifths of rural Mexico lives in poverty, over half in extreme poverty.

- Imports surpass exports, leaving Mexico with a serious global balance-of-trade deficit.

- The environment has deteriorated. The Mexican government estimates that the economic costs of environmental degradation have amounted to 10% of annual GDP [gross domestic product], or $36 billion per year. These costs dwarf economic growth, which amounted to only $9.4 billion annually.

In many ways, Mexico got what NAFTA promised: trade and investment. Unfortunately, these have not translated into benefits for the Mexican population as a whole or into improvements in the country's fragile environment. The Mexican experience reminds us that increased trade and investment should not be the end objectives of economic integration. Instead, they should be considered as possible means to improve social welfare and environmental quality.

The Crisis in the Countryside

Mexico's national organization of basic grains farmers (ANEC) and the State Coalition of Coffee Producers of Oaxaca (CEPCO) have been living a free trade nightmare for years. They now are among the leading members of Mexico's resurgent farmers' movement, which recently mobilized broad support for the demand to renegotiate NAFTA's agricultural provisions and won important concessions on agricultural policy from the [then-president Vicente] Fox administration. They represent contrasting experiences, since grain farmers produce mainly for the domestic market and face direct competition from more developed and highly subsidized U.S. producers, while coffee farmers produce for export and have no U.S. competitors. Today, however, ANEC's 180,000 members and CEPCO's 30,000 indigenous farmer families find themselves similarly impoverished, abandoned by the Mexican government to global markets suffering overproduction, low prices, and domination by a small number of transnational buyers.

When NAFTA was negotiated, Mexico's leaders promised the agreement would help modernize the countryside, converting low-yield peasant plots into highly productive commercial farms growing fruits, vegetables, and other export crops for the U.S. market. Farmers who could not modernize or export would be absorbed as workers into the rising export industrial sector. Sensitive to the important role of corn in Mexico's culture and economy, NAFTA included 10-to-15-year tariff phase-out periods for corn and other basic grains, along with strict import quotas, with the goal of ensuring a gradual

Farmers Take to Streets Over New NAFTA Rules

Anti-NAFTA protests have been a regular occurrence in Mexico, with farmers riding into the Congress building in Mexico City on horseback and blocking roads leading south from the capital last December [2002].

At least a dozen campesino organizations, along with environmental groups and others, have formed a coalition called the "Countryside Can't Take it Anymore" to fight for the survival of Mexico's rural life.... The 25 million people who live in rural areas, where 20 percent of Mexican jobs are located, are struggling for their very survival.

Stephen Leahy,
Inter Press Service,
January 3, 2003.

transition to international competition with more developed and highly subsidized U.S. producers.

Farmers were confronted with a far different reality. The Mexican government, citing supply shortages for basic grains, unilaterally approved imports from the United States over NAFTA's quotas and then declined to collect tariffs. The result was free trade shock treatment for grain farmers: Instead of a difficult long-term adjustment to competition with U.S. farmers they faced the near-impossible challenge of fully liberalized trade just three years into NAFTA. Imports surged and prices fell nearly 50%. At the same time, the Mexican government ended its price-support system. Facing fiscal pressures after the peso crisis and bailout of the banking sector, the government also reduced other rural support and modernization programs.

Farmers Fight Back

ANEC responded with an aggressive effort to keep small farmers on the land. It bought abandoned state storage facilities, developed its own marketing infrastructure, promoted regional trade between surplus and deficit states, distributed risk among its members in the absence of crop insurance programs, promoted sustainable agriculture practices, and earned 10% to 12% higher prices for its members. But producers still face low prices, high imports, and inadequate government support.

Small coffee farmers suffered a similar fate, despite producing for export. In their case, the culprit was the free trade bias against worldwide supply management of commodities, which is proscribed by international agreements. Faced with falling prices and abandonment by the government, CEPCO and other farmer organizations, like ANEC, showed precisely the kind of self-reliant collective entrepreneurship development specialists dream of. They adapted to the harsh new market conditions, evolved larger and more powerful forms of organization, achieved greater economies of scale, took advantage of new opportunities afforded by the liberalization process, capitalized their operations through well-considered acquisitions of state production facilities, and created new markets under changing conditions.

By all accounts, these efforts are exemplary. They also are clearly inadequate, absent a stronger state role in promoting the sectors' development. The new farmers' movement demanded but failed to win the renegotiation of NAFTA's chapter on agriculture, although it garnered some increases in government commitments to rural development. The movement also asserted Mexico's right to food security and sovereignty: the ability to ensure adequate access to safe foods produced domestically.

Exploitation and Expulsion

The free trade model in Mexico is designed to take advantage of Mexico's comparative advantage in low wages, with the country's decades-old *maquiladora* [factory] export assembly sector as the engine for industrial development. For Mexican workers, this has meant two things: exploitation and expulsion.

Mexico trades on its low-wage economy, and it has failed to guarantee basic labor rights in the process, despite NAFTA's labor side agreement. Consider the determined campaign for worker rights in the Autotrim maquiladora in Matamoros, Tamaulipas. Just across the border from Brownsville, Texas, Matamoros has seen significant growth with NAFTA and the expansion of the export assembly sector. Autotrim is one of the many auto parts plants that subcontract work for U.S. automakers, employing 1,400 workers in the production of leather coverings for steering wheels and gear shifts. Since 1992 workers have mobilized without success for independent union representation and improved health and safety practices at the plant.

Worker demands initially focused on health and safety problems, which included repetitive motion injuries, exposures to toxic solvents and glues, and a pattern of birth defects among workers' babies. Such conditions are not unusual in the sector. One survey found that 60% of Matamoros' 60,000 *maquiladora* workers reported injuries or other health problems related to their work. The responses of company representatives and leaders of the government-affiliated union at the plant were also typical: They denied the claims and refused to address the conditions.

The resulting struggle for independent union representation saw mass firings by the company and intimidation by the government-affiliated union. When workers linked up with their counterparts at other Mexican plants and at a Canadian plant owned by the same company in an impressive show of cross-border organizing, the result was the closure of the Canadian plant. Finally, the Mexican workers took their complaints to the National Administrative Office, the body created by NAFTA's side agreement to guarantee labor rights. The eventual finding in the workers' favor—after long and damaging delays—was welcome but revealed the weakness of the accord. It acknowledged the justice of the workers' demands, but there have been no significant changes in labor representation or health and safety at Autotrim as a direct result of the decision.

Meanwhile, widespread layoffs in the *maquiladoras* and many other sectors of the economy have caused a rising stream of migrants searching for work in Mexico or in the United States, where North America's better job opportunities lie. . . .

Learning NAFTA's Lessons

The Mexican government wholeheartedly chose the free trade path for development. It is now clear where that path has led: declining living standards, a degraded environment, and a government that does not address the basic needs of its citizens.

This is one of NAFTA's many lessons. The Mexican government not only opened its economy to U.S. goods, services, and capital, it also followed the accompanying prescription to reduce the government's involvement in the economy. It thus abdicated its developmental responsibilities to the whims of the market. . . . The market will not guarantee that economic activity benefits the citizenry, promotes sustainable practices, or addresses national priorities. Only a strong government can set development priorities, regulate private activity for the public good, enact and enforce environmental and labor standards, and protect those areas of social and economic activity deemed to be of strategic importance.

Nor can governments allow the search for export markets to preclude the strengthening of the internal market. Mexico needs both foreign investment and foreign markets, but the current model undermines the country's economic foundations. Some of the country's largest sources of employment, such as small farms and small- and medium-sized enterprises, have been weakened by economic integration. As recent farmers' movement demands have emphasized, government investment is needed in important areas to which foreign investors are not attracted. And governments need to retain the power to impose some performance requirements on investors to ensure investment serves national development goals. Such measures are largely proscribed by NAFTA and other trade agreements, to the detriment of sustained national economic development in the global South.

| *"In principle, free trade and fair trade can go hand in hand, and offer the best chance of... prosperity."*

Fair-Trade Policies Can Help Developing Nations

Martin Vander Weyer

Free trade generally benefits poorer countries, but that does not mean that that trade is always fair, asserts Martin Vander Weyer in the following viewpoint. Rich countries often protect their industries with tariffs or subsidies for domestic agricultural products, he notes, and at times, trade may present a moral dilemma; for example, should European powers favor their ex-colonies whose economies were shaped by the policies of colonial days? Despite complications, Vander Weyer holds that overall, trade is good, and that rich countries should seek to create a more even playing field between the rich and poor nations. Martin Vander Weyer is business editor for the British magazine the Spectator *and the author of* Falling Eagle: The Decline of Barclay's Bank.

As you read, consider the following questions:

1. Where does Vander Weyer say the World Trade Organization is headquartered?

Martin Vander Weyer, "Can Free Trade Be Fair Trade?" *New Statesman*, vol. 134, February 28, 2005. Copyright © 2005 New Statesman, Ltd. Reproduced by permission.

2. What is the one example given by the author of a country or area that "wholeheartedly" practiced free trade?

3. In the view of Martin Wolf, as cited by Vander Weyer, how do factories designed to produce goods for Western markets help the Bangladeshi women who work in them?

Free and fair are words that often go together, like spick and span or Marks & Spencer. Free and fair elections, for example, are events devoutly to be wished for everywhere from Baghdad to your local town hall. But what of free trade and fair trade? Do they go hand in hand, or is one the enemy of the other?

Contrasting Views of Trade

The loose alliance of anti-globalisation protesters and fair-trade campaigners who subscribe to the view—expressed on a banner displayed during the Seattle protests [at the 1999 World Trade Organisation summit]—that capitalism should be replaced by "something nicer", clearly takes the latter view. To them, free trade is a conspiracy of the rich to get richer at the expense of the poor, with the World Trade Organisation [WTO]—the Geneva-based, 148-member Tower of Babel that sets the rules—doing the dirty work on behalf of Washington and its corporate cronies. In the free traders' dark heart, the protesters claim, is a plot to steal the developing world's natural resources, wreck its environment and treat its workers like slaves while ensuring that [corporate giant] Halliburton gets the infrastructure contracts, McDonald's gets the fast-food franchises and the World Bank gets its loans back.

By contrast, a line of reputable laissez-faire thinkers from Adam Smith to the *Financial Times*'s Martin Wolf take the former view: that international trade without the interference of tariffs, subsidies, price controls and pork-barrel politics is by far the most efficient way of matching global supply to de-

mand while making all the participants more prosperous—
and that the best indicator of fairness in a broad sense is rising prosperity, the absence of which makes all the benefits of
a just and well-ordered society so much harder to obtain.
Crucial to this side of the argument is the idea that, as [Brit-
ish economist] John Kay put it in his even-handed analysis
The Truth About Markets (2003): "We who live in rich states
are not rich because those who live in poor states are
poor"—or [satirist] PJ O'Rourke, rather less even-handedly in
Eat the Rich (1998): "Economics is not zero-sum. If you eat
too many slices of pizza, I don't have to eat the box."

Truly Free Trade Is Rare

You might expect George W Bush to subscribe to the right-
wing O'Rourke's school, even if you suspect that he under-
stands diddly-squat about economics.

Here is what he said shortly after he became president in
2001: "Open trade is not just an economic opportunity, it is a
moral imperative." But what did he do in March 2002 to drum
up Republican support in "rust-belt" states for the midterm
congressional elections? He whacked a 30 per cent tariff on
steel imports, causing extreme pain to exporters in parts of
the world with which the US was supposed to be friendly, including Britain, Japan, South Korea and Vladimir Putin's Russia. When Russia responded in kind by banning imports of
US poultry, jeopardising jobs in 38 states, Bush stuck to his
guns, because the steel votes outnumbered the chicken votes.
And when pressure from the WTO and other factors—including the need for alliance-building for "the war on terror"—
made it expedient to take the steel tariff off again, he declared
the whole episode a victory against anti-competitive practices
in world trade.

Therein lies the problem in trying to judge whether free
trade is fair. Like socialism, it has hardly ever been put into

practice wholeheartedly; purists have to look back to Hong Kong in the 1960s for an example.

Politicians pay lip-service to the social and economic benefits of open markets and are always ready to lecture other countries about it. But they invariably back away as soon as jobs and votes are threatened at home.

Subsidies and Favoritism

And when it comes to agriculture (with the exception of subsidy-free New Zealand), politicians do not even bother to pay lip-service. In 2000, every cow in the European Union [EU] received the equivalent of $913 in subsidy, while every sub-Saharan African received $8 in EU aid. Two-fifths of the entire EU budget goes on subsidising farmers and putting food producers everywhere else in the world at an unfair disadvantage—except possibly American farmers, who are themselves comfortably protected by a $180 [billion] subsidy deal also brought in by George W Bush in 2002.

Yet we must also be fair to politicians: sometimes they must find the morality of free and fair trade genuinely confusing. Take the story of the humble banana, staple product of several of Britain's former Caribbean dependencies and of Latin America's so-called "banana republics", such as Ecuador, which fall within America's sphere of influence. For many years, Caribbean producers enjoyed privileged access to EU markets, while Latin American "dollar bananas" were subject to hefty tariffs and quotas. But small traditional farmers in the Windward Islands tended to produce small, expensive fruits, while big, efficient operations in Ecuador produced big, cheap ones. The Latin producers already had a large slice of the European market (Germans like their bananas big) but wanted more, and argued with some justification that they were being blatantly discriminated against.

The WTO and the [Bill] Clinton administration agreed with them—and the US threatened punitive tariffs on a list of luxury goods, including Scottish cashmere knitwear and "tartan" shortbread, unless the EU moved swiftly to remove the barrier. An open-and-shut case, you might think, but there were other factors muddying the water—not least that Carl H Lindner, the tycoon behind the Chiquita company of Cincinnati which controls most of the Latin American banana trade, happened to be one of Bill Clinton's major campaign contributors.

If you were a trade minister, would you think it fairer to stick up for old-fashioned Commonwealth preference[1] (it was, after all, we colonialists who converted these island economies to banana production in the first place) or for Ecuadorian farmers who had for so long been denied equal market access? The outcome so far has been a long foot-dragging exercise, in which the EU has provided aid to convert Caribbean producers to other crops, but dollar bananas are still subject to higher duties; yet another "trade war" looms as a result.

Factories Bring Progress for Women

Or take another issue that stirs strong emotions: the exploitation of labour in poor countries—very often women and children—to produce cheap goods for export to rich countries. Martin Wolf tackles this one in *Why Globalisation Works* (2004), using the example of Bangladeshi women in the clothing industry. Is it morally wrong of us to buy shirts made in vile factories paying pittance wages?

No, it isn't, Wolf argues: before these factories came along to meet western demand, tradition forbade women from such work; now they have "a measure of autonomy" and their wages make it possible for a higher proportion of family incomes to be spent on education, health and nutrition. To western eyes their conditions look dreadful, but compared to the alterna-

1. The Commonwealth of Nations comprises more than fifty countries, many former British colonies, in a voluntary association headed by the monarch of England. Traditionally, these member countries have given trade preferences to other members.

Preferential Access

The 79 countries of the African-Caribbean-Pacific (ACP) grouping, mainly former European colonies, have for decades enjoyed preferential access to European markets, a legacy of imperial trade arrangements. They face lower—frequently zero—tariffs selling into the EU than those encountered by most other developing countries. For some producers, such as Namibian and Botswana cattle farmers, this preferential treatment is the difference between being able to sell into the European market at all and being swamped by more efficient producers from the likes of Brazil and Argentina. . . .

A fierce debate has developed over whether these trade deals will do much to help the ACP countries or, because ACP governments are required to open their own markets to European goods in return, the pacts merely represent traditional EU "mercantilist" export promotion. Is all of this, in other words, a continuation of the colonial relationship rather than an attempt to escape from it?

Alan Beattie and Andrew Bounds,
Commonwealth Secretariat, December 17, 2007.

tives—dependency as a wife or despised daughter, prostitution, farm labour, begging—the factories offer "enormous gains". Taking a stance against this kind of trade development, he says, is "mere tokenism. To be upset over poverty is entirely justifiable; to block a route out of it, in response, is not".

Free Trade Can Be Fair Trade

In the end, most economists tend to agree with Wolf that developing countries gain more in terms of social progress and eradication of poverty when they engage more openly in international trade, while countries that do not do so—North Korea springs to mind—get left behind. Protectionism and closed borders encourage corruption, inefficiency and lack of opportunity; trade and inward investment encourage technology transfer, rising standards and rising aspirations.

For sure, there are bad foreign-owned factories in Dhaka and Jakarta, and rapacious middlemen in the Kenyan coffee trade; for sure also, western governments have been shamelessly hypocritical in protecting their own markets, and the WTO has yet to prove itself a true friend to the poor. But in principle, free trade and fair trade can go hand in hand, and offer the best chance of a slice of the pizza of prosperity.

> "A troubling gap lies between the purported benefits of Fair Trade and reality."

The Benefits of Fair-Trade Policies Are Often Illusory

Jeremy Weber

Jeremy Weber is a graduate student in the Agricultural and Applied Economics Department at the University of Wisconsin–Madison. In the following viewpoint, Weber highlights some of the differences between what consumers believe about "fair trade" coffee and actual practice in coffee-producing regions. He also points out instances where the fair-trade campaign is actually hurting the very people it is supposed to help: marginalized and small-scale coffee producers. For the campaign for fair trade to benefit a large number of farmers, Weber maintains, those involved in the fair trade movement must change their attitude toward business and the free market.

As you read, consider the following questions:

1. What are some examples given by Weber of differences between "fair trade" coffee drinkers' beliefs and the actual rules under the fair-trade standard?

Jeremy Weber, "Fair Trade Coffee Enthusiasts Should Confront Reality," *Cato Journal*, Winter 2007, pp. 109–116. This article has been excerpted and edited for this publication.

2. Why is the increasing demand for organic coffee in the fair-trade market a problem for small coffee growers, in the author's view?

3. According to Weber, how must fair-trade advocates change their ideology in order to make the campaign a widespread success?

From university cafeterias to supermarkets in the developed world, people are buying Fair Trade (FT) coffee certified by the FLO-Cert, the certifying entity of Fairtrade Labelling Organizations International (FLO). The assumption is that such purchases will contribute to the welfare of marginalized producers in the developing world. While sales of FT coffee in Europe have stabilized, the North American and Japanese markets are growing rapidly. Total sales increased 40 percent from 2004 to 2005, to a total volume of 33,992 metric tons (MT).

Defining "Fair Trade"

What is "Fair Trade"? According to FINE, the umbrella organization that comprises the four largest Fair Trade organizations (FLO, International Federation for Alternative Trade, Network of European World Shops, and the European Fair Trade Association)

> Fair Trade is a trading partnership, based on dialogue, transparency and respect, that seeks greater equity in international trade. It contributes to sustainable development by offering better trading conditions to, and securing the rights of, marginalized producers and workers—especially in the South.

The FINE definition optimistically assumes that the trading partnerships and conditions promoted by Fair Trade necessarily "contribute to sustainable development." It is true that the Fair Trade coffee system—the producers, exporters, importers, and retailers operating by the rules and standards of FLO—has improved living standards for many participating coffee growers. Yet the system faces vexing issues such as a disconnect between promotional materials and reality, excess supply, and the marginalization of economically disadvantaged producers and groups. Those involved in Fair Trade coffee debates and governance must address these issues if Fair Trade is to be an effective mechanism for rural development in coffee producing regions.

The Search for Culprits

Unfortunately, many of those close to the movement prefer to blame profit-seeking corporations for hijacking Fair Trade instead of objectively analyzing the workings of the Fair Trade coffee system. For example, the financial manager of a Peruvian Fair Trade coffee exporter explained to me that his company's critique of FLO is that it will allow companies like Nestlé to participate, even though such companies are only in Fair Trade for the profit. Never mind that the company he works for is a privately owned, for-profit export company. As [economics theorist] Adam Smith so well noted, the interest of the merchants (including coffee exporters) is always to narrow the competition and expand the market. Likewise, the executive director of a major retailer of Fair Trade coffee assured me that the problem with Fair Trade is the participation of too many ideologically uncommitted entities. Even though this director was new to the job and had never visited a Fair Trade coffee cooperative, he had already determined the cause of the problem. This knee-jerk, blame-greedy-corporations reaction is common among Fair Trade enthusiasts. At the 2nd International Fair Trade Colloquium held in Montreal in June of 2006 the hot topic was the participation of large corporations in the Fair Trade coffee system.

Promotional Materials vs. Reality

While the participation of large transnational companies may alter the dynamics of the Fair Trade coffee system, Fair Trade faces more serious practical issues. A large gap divides the story depicted by Fair Trade marketing materials from the standards of FLO and the advantages of producer participation. This misleading representation of Fair Trade has led many socially conscious coffee drinkers to hold unexamined assumptions about the benefits of Fair Trade.

In trying to boost sales many retailers claim that Fair Trade coffee guarantees a living wage to coffee growers. A major promoter of Fair Trade coffee, Global Exchange, states on its website, "Fair Trade guarantees to poor farmers organized in cooperatives around the world: a living wage." While it remains to be seen what constitutes a "living wage," in reality, Fair Trade guarantees nothing to producers. Fair Trade ensures a minimum price to *organizations* of producers, but not to individual producers. The organization serves as an intermediary between the producer and the market. Producers receive the price stipulated in the organization's export contract, which must meet or exceed the Fair Trade minimum price, minus the expenses of the organization. Since Fair Trade eliminates "unnecessary" intermediaries, producer organizations must perform the tasks previously conducted by those intermediaries. In this arrangement, an organization must obtain financing to buy coffee from its members, sort and process coffee, and coordinate export logistics. Each of those activities generates expenses which, if not managed effectively and efficiently, can consume much of the higher Fair Trade price before it reaches growers. In some cases, organizations' export costs have been high enough to induce member producers to sell to the local market instead of to their organization for the Fair Trade market.

Poorly Paid Workers

Many Fair Trade coffee drinkers also believe that hired laborers on a Fair Trade certified coffee farm receive a minimum wage of some sort. In the case of coffee sold by producer organizations, wage standards only apply to employees of the organization. Specific standards regarding temporary workers hired by coffee farmers do not exist. Most hired labor on small-scale coffee farms, however, is seasonal. Standards for small farmers' organizations state, "Where workers are casually hired by farmers themselves, the organizations should take steps to improve working conditions and to ensure that such workers share the benefits of Fair Trade." Hal Weitzman of the *Financial Times* visited five Fair Trade farms in northern Peru and found that four of the farms paid workers below the Peruvian minimum wage.

Such payments do not violate Fair Trade standards. In its response to the Weitzman article, the Fair Trade Foundation reiterated its norms regarding workers hired by small-scale producers and recognized "that the members of these producer organisations are small farmers who struggle to earn a decent livelihood for themselves and their families." Unfortunately, Fair Trade promotional materials have lured coffee drinkers into believing that Fair Trade guarantees farmers and workers a fair or living wage, which most consumers probably interpret to mean a wage at or above the legal minimum in the coffee-producing country. . . .

Costly Certification

With an excess supply of coffee, the Fair Trade market has increasingly demanded organic coffee. The dual certification of Fair Trade and organic has allowed coffee organizations to differentiate their coffee in a saturated market. Between 1996 and 2000, exports of dual certified coffee (Fair Trade and organic) grew from 86.25 MT to 5,096 MT, an increase of about 5,800 percent. According to Fair Trade fast facts, approximately 85 percent of Fair Trade coffee sold in the United States is certified organic.

Quality standards have risen significantly since 2000. Furthermore, beginning in 2004 FLO began charging producer organizations $3,200 to become certified. These increasing demands are easily understood when viewed in a market context of excess supply. In other words, barriers to entering the Fair Trade market have intensified to equilibrate supply and demand in a market with a price floor.

Entry barriers affect who participates in the market. Entering the Fair Trade coffee market, especially the Fair Trade organic market, presents major difficulties for young producer organizations. Without assistance from development organizations or export companies, the very organizations and producers that Fair Trade targets have little chance of participating in the market. Obtaining the certification of the FLO requires someone within the organization to coordinate the involved certification process. The soliciting organization must also obtain an export contract and the necessary financing to buy and export coffee. Most organizations need around $15,000 in financing to export one container of Fair Trade coffee. . . .

Since the Fair Trade coffee market is consistently demanding more and more organic coffee, many organizations find that they must become organic certified to obtain export contracts. The organic certification process is more expensive and demanding than that of FLO. Most organic certification programs last three years. Each year requires an external inspection from the certifying entity. An external inspection for an organization of 100 producers can generally cost around $2,000. The more significant cost, however, is in providing technical assistance in organic production norms to participating farmers. The total cost of implementing an organic certification program in four Peruvian coffee organizations ranged from $300 to more than $1,000 per producer.

Increased barriers to entry have made it increasingly difficult for marginalized producers, which Fair Trade supposedly targets, to participate. As in most industries, increasing barriers to entry benefits those already established in the market. Such is the case in the Fair Trade coffee market, which is

More Harm than Good

[Tim Wilson, a research fellow at Australia's Institute of Public Affairs, noted that] there was evidence that Fairtrade products could do more harm than good for coffee producers in undeveloped nations. He cited reports alleging producers had been charged thousands of dollars to become certified Fairtrade providers and some labourers received as little as $3 a day.

Caroline Overington,
Australian, April 28, 2007.

dominated primarily by those privileged groups who entered the market in its less competitive days. The Fair Trade model based on a minimum price will inevitably produce a tension between concentrating market shares to a few groups, which leaves many out of the Fair Trade system, and distributing market shares to many groups, which results in each producer selling only a fraction of his production to the Fair Trade market.

Getting Comfortable with the Market

A troubling gap lies between the purported benefits of Fair Trade and reality. Nevertheless, participation in Fair Trade networks has undoubtedly generated benefits for many producers. Integrating new producer groups into Fair Trade, however, depends on the size of the market. Ironically, the most obvious way to increase coffee sales, enlisting the resources of mainstream coffee retailers, is seen by many enthusiasts as the biggest threat facing Fair Trade. The ideal of the Fair Trade movement is the participation of entities whose business is 100 percent Fair Trade certified. In reality, Starbucks is the largest purchaser of Fair Trade coffee in North America although Fair Trade coffee only comprises 3.7 percent of the company's purchases.

Sue Mecklenburg, the vice president of sustainable procurement for Starbucks, believes that a pressing question is, "Can Fair Trade get comfortable in the competitive market?" The size of the Fair Trade coffee market and the competitiveness of the entities that link producers to the market affect Fair Trade's ability to generate benefits for producers. As stated previously, poor management of the export process by producer organizations can consume much of the higher Fair Trade price before it reaches growers. Some producer organizations such as APROECO in Peru have entered partnerships with companies to capitalize on the scale and expertise of private export companies. APROECO's relationship with a private export company also allowed the organization to overcome the entry barriers of the Fair Trade and organic markets (e.g., certification and contractual costs). A study of Costa Rican coffee mills by Loraine Ronchi of the World Bank suggests that such partnerships may increase prices paid to farmers. The study found that Fair Trade cooperative mills had lower price markdowns (defined as the difference between the price paid to mills and the price that mills paid to coffee farmers) than non-Fair Trade, nonforeign-owned mills. At the same time, vertically integrated multinational mills had a similar effect of lowering price markdowns when compared with nonforeign-owned mills. FLO should welcome partnerships between producer organizations and private companies instead of insisting that producer organizations assume all export responsibilities. Social justice goals and efficiency can complement each other.

If Fair Trade is dominated by those who see mainstream for-profit companies as intrinsically destructive, the movement will remain a fringe, niche market that supports a few privileged groups. Fair Trade enthusiasts must spend more time asking hard, practical questions about how Fair Trade functions and less time searching for enemies. Only with a strong dose of practicality and self-critique can the Fair Trade movement create an effective mechanism for promoting development in coffee-producing communities.

Periodical Bibliography

The following articles have been selected to supplement the diverse views presented in this chapter.

Ha-Joon Chang
"Kicking Away the Ladder: Infant Industry Promotion in Historical Perspective," *Oxford Development Studies*, vol. 31, no. 1, 2003.

Peter Coy
"Why Free Trade Talks Are in Free Fall," *Business Week Online*, 2006. www.business week.com.

Kevin P. Gallagher
"Is NAFTA Working for Mexico?" *Environmental Forum*, May 2006.

Government Accounting Office
"International Trade: Mexico's Maquiladora Decline Affects U.S.-Mexico Border Communities and Trade; Recovery Depends in Part on Mexico's Actions," *GAO Reports*, GAO-03-891, 2003.

Peter Hardstaff
"We Need Trade Justice, Not Free Trade," *New Statesman*, February 26, 2007.

Ethan B. Kapstein
"The New Global Slave Trade," *Foreign Affairs*, November-December 2006.

Homi Kharas
"Lifting All Boats," *Foreign Policy*, January-February 2005.

Manuel F. Montes and Swarnim Wagle
"Why Asia Needs to Trade Smarter," *Far Eastern Economic Review*, June 2006.

Diego Sanchez-Ancochea
"Trade Liberalization and Economic Integration in the Americas: Causes and Consequences," *Latin American Politics & Society*, Summer 2006.

Andrew Small
"Global Trade and the Common Good," *America*, December 12, 2005.

OPPOSING
VIEWPOINTS®
SERIES

CHAPTER 3

How Does Free Trade Affect Labor and the Environment?

Chapter Preface

Concerns over the effects of free trade on the environment and on labor standards are felt in both the developed and the developing worlds. Opponents of free trade argue that free trade will encourage a "race to the bottom" in the way workers and nature are treated. Free-trade advocates argue that trade creates prosperity, and prosperity creates better working conditions and more effective environmental regulations.

Labor rights and wages are a primary concern of those who believe that free trade leads to a race to the bottom. One of the main culprits, in their eyes, is China. Alan Tonelson, an author and lobbyist for American industry, sees the lack of labor rights in that country as being detrimental to American workers and firms:

> China has no labor unions. There are no labor rights in China, so that when Chinese workers have problems, they have no option of going to management or going to their union to get help.... China also has an enormous unemployment rate, so there is a big surplus of labor in China, and that alone keeps workers well-behaved because everybody is afraid of losing their job.

Supporters of free trade counter that work in a modern factory is both more pleasant and better paid than work on a small farm; in China and most other Asian countries workers for new plants come from the countryside, leaving behind arduous agricultural work. The economist Charles Wheelan, in his book *Naked Economics*, notes that

> [Athletic shoe manufacturer] Nike does not use forced labor in its Vietnamese factories. Why are workers willing to accept a dollar or two a day? *Because it is better than any other option they have.* According to the Institute for International

Economics, the average wage paid by foreign companies in low-income countries is twice the average domestic manufacturing wage.

The disagreement over labor standards is matched by a controversy over environmental regulations. Those opposed to free trade believe that developing-world countries might become "pollution havens" for industries seeking to avoid tough environmental regulations in developed nations. Free traders point to the Environmental Kuznet's Curve (EKC), an economic theory that suggests that as income goes up in a country, so does environmental regulation. As trade would increase income in the developing world, they argue, it would eventually help lead to better environmental regulation.

The evidence so far is mixed. When the U.S. government was debating the North American Free Trade Agreement (NAFTA) in the early 1990s, there was concern that Mexico would become a pollution haven. It has not, according to economist Kevin P. Gallagher of Tufts University's Global Development and Environment Institute. It has not happened because Mexico's chief advantage in trade is having an abundance of low-cost labor, not lax environmental regulations. At the same time, the environment has not improved, as predicted by the EKC theory, despite the country's economy reaching the predicted "turning point" in national income at which environmental improvement is said to become a priority of government and the society overall. As Professor Stephen Mumme of Colorado State University writes:

> It is now plain that NAFTA's rules protecting trade and investment in the trinational region are an invitation to the private sector to challenge environmental regulations. These rules and their implementation procedures must be shored up if a gradual erosion of state and provincial standards is to be avoided.

The debate remains unresolved. Will Chinese labor standards improve? If they do, will international firms simply relocate to another country with even cheaper labor? Will Mexico implement improved environmental regulation? Or are developing countries simply less concerned about environmental issues? This chapter's viewpoints address these questions.

> "Each country must decide for itself what the optimal combination of trade and environmental policies suits it best."

Free Trade Can Lead to Both Economic Growth and Environmental Improvement

B. Delworth Gardner

B. Delworth Gardner is professor emeritus of agricultural economics at the University of California at Davis and a fellow at the Property and Environmental Resources Center. He has been a consultant to the Agency for International Development and the California Water Resources Board. In the following viewpoint, Gardner summarizes the work of social scientists who study the relation between trade, economic growth, and environmental conditions contends that there is no evidence that free trade leads to a "race-to-the-bottom" in which countries cut environmental regulations in order to attract investment by heavily polluting industries.

B. Delworth Gardner, *You Have to Admit It's Getting Better: From Economic Prosperity to Environmental Quality*. Stanford, CA: Hoover Institution Press, 2004, pp. 116–123. Copyright © 2004 by the Board of Trustees of the Leland Stanford Junior University. Reproduced by permission.

As you read, consider the following questions:

1. What does Gardner describe as statistician Bjørn Lomborg's evidence that the environment is improving due to free trade?
2. What is a "debt-for-nature" swap, as described by the author?
3. What effect does Gardner assert an increase in income has on a nation's level of pollution?

The nexus between international trade and environmental quality is more complex than appears at first blush. Three connections will be explored in this [viewpoint]: (1) increases in incomes and demand for environmental quality; (2) direct trading in environmental goods; and (3) indirect effects of trade on environmental regulation and technical change.

Income and Environmental Quality

If free trade unambiguously increases average per-capita income . . . , what can be said about the relationship between the level and growth of income and environmental quality?

A major contribution to what is known about trade and the environment is [statistician] Bjørn Lomborg's outstanding book *The Skeptical Environmentalist*. Lomborg's first chapter, "Things Are Getting Better," is a comprehensive survey of the current state of the world's environment. Lomborg uses the same indicators and data sources as those utilized by prominent "green" organizations whose allegations include an increasing population overrunning the capacity of the world to feed itself; falling levels of human health; shrinking forests; eroding soils; declining water quality; falling groundwater tables; disappearing wetlands; collapsing fisheries; deteriorating rangelands; rising world temperatures; dying coral reefs; and disappearing plant and animal species. In a *tour de force*, Lomborg demonstrates that fears of these deteriorating conditions are unfounded—instead of the environment getting worse, it is actually improving in nearly all respects.

Lomborg also indicates why this improvement is occurring. Trade and less costly transport effectively act to reduce risks and make local areas less vulnerable to natural resource exhaustion and depletion. This is a tremendously important insight. In a trading economy; production does not necessarily have to take place at the physical location of demand, but where it is most efficient. An implication is that as resource scarcity occurs and prices and costs rise in a trading world, production will shift to other locations with less scarcity and lower prices and costs. The effect is that each country can almost indefinitely postpone running into a wall imposed by resource scarcity, and all of the trading economies will benefit.

Lomborg makes another salient point: "We have grown to believe that we are faced with an inescapable choice between higher economic welfare and a greener environment. But, surprisingly. . . environmental development often stems from economic development—only when we get sufficiently rich can we afford the relative luxury of caring about the environment."

Direct Trade in Environmental Goods

Another way that international trade and the environment are related is through direct trading in environmental goods, such as debt-for-nature swaps and pollution-emission rights, both of which have become prominent in the past two decades. Gains from trade may be large because of differences among countries in their endowments of nature and in their preferences for environmental goods.

A debt-for-nature swap typically involves three or more parties: an international conservation organization (such as the Nature Conservancy or the WWF [World Wildlife Federation]), a conservation organization from the country where the conservation work is to be done (host country),

Development Is Key to Protecting Environment

Most forms of environmental pollution look as though they have either been exaggerated or are transient—associated with the early phases of industrialization. . . .

The focus should be on development, not sustainability. Development is not simply valuable in itself, but in the long run it will lead the third world to become more concerned about the environment. Only when people are rich enough to feed themselves do they begin to think about the effect of their actions on the world around them and on future generations.

Bjørn Lomborg, New York Times, *August 26, 2002.*

and one or more government agencies in the host country. The international conservation organization desires to maintain or improve the environment in the host country and is willing to pay because its members place high value on environmental amenities. The host-country conservation organization has the interest and presumed competence needed to manage a conservation project, and the host-country governmental organizations facilitate the transfer of the debt, for a price, and will generally disburse the funds.

The process ordinarily begins when the debtor country's central bank agrees to sell some of its external debt, usually because the country has a problem generating foreign exchange and does not have the hard currency to pay its foreign debts. The international environmental organization can often acquire the debt at a significant discount, especially if it is willing to take the proceeds in the currency of the host country—no problem, since the host country is where the expenditures for environmental improvement will occur.

A swap normally requires that the host country place domestic currency bonds in an environmental trust fund held in the country's central bank where the funds will be at the disposal of the international conservation organization and disbursed to the host-country conservation organization. . . .

Direct trading for the right to emit pollutants among countries also has potential for reducing the costs of international agreements to control pollution. The Kyoto Protocol, for example, specifies emission targets for each participant developed country (the developing countries were exempted from the agreement). The protocol also establishes, however, the possibility of trading rights for carbon dioxide emissions that might affect the atmosphere of all countries. Countries would be given allowances to emit carbon dioxide, but then could buy and sell these rights at a negotiated price. All trading countries could be made better off in trading pollution rights to those countries in which the costs of reducing emissions are highest. Lomborg cites studies showing that the cost of the Kyoto Protocol would be $346 billion a year with no trades in emission rights, whereas with trade permitted among the rich countries the cost drops to $161 billion annually. If trade were global among all countries, the aggregate cost would be even lower, at $75 billion. Since these potential gains are so large, trading markets would surely arise and institutions would surely be fashioned to accommodate them. The United States argued strongly for this trading strategy but has withdrawn from the protocol, so perhaps the most powerful advocate for emissions trading within the protocol is now gone.

Environmental Regulation and Technical Change

A seminal paper by [economists Werner] Antweiler, [Brian R.] Copeland, and [M. Scott] Taylor provides convincing theoretical and empirical evidence that international trade is good for the environment. They postulate that trade affects environmental quality through three channels: (1) the location of production; (2) the scale of production; and (3) the techniques of production. Their econometric model estimates the independent effects of each of these channels on variation in the concentrations of sulfur dioxide in the air among the countries sampled. Changes in the location of production attributable to international trade are found to be empirically trivial. Freer trade results in an increase in the scale of production, and this effect has a modest negative impact on environmental quality (more output is associated with a little more pollution). A 1 percent increase in the scale of production raises pollution concentrations by 0.25 to 0.5 percent for an average country in the sample. It is the increase in income produced by trade liberalization that is the dominating force, driving concentrations of pollutants down by a significant amount (1.25 to 1.5 percent) via the technique effect. The critical explanatory factor is that wealthier countries value environmental amenities more highly and enhance their production by employing environmentally friendly technologies.

The findings of this study are in sharp contrast to what some of the most vocal opponents of globalization and free trade believe, which is that if companies are to be internationally competitive as free trade requires, governments have no choice but to dismantle health, safety, and environmental regulations. In the language of the day, international competition induces a "regulatory race to the bottom." . . .

No "Race-to-the-Bottom"

[Economist and development expert] Jagdish Bhagwati argues that although the race-to-the-bottom argument may be theoretically valid, it fails on empirical grounds. Little evidence exists that governments actually play the competitive game by offering to cut standards or that multinational corporations are seduced by such concessions.

Indeed, most recent trade agreements affirm the right of each country to choose its own level of environmental protection. The North American Free Trade Agreement (NAFTA), for example, specifically provides that no member country should relax its health, safety, and environmental standards for the purpose of attracting or retaining investment in its territory. Moreover, arbitration tribunals are established specifically to referee protests and conflict, including those in the environmental arena.

What about the possibility that national governments competing for trade will be less inclined to pass and enforce environmental standards, given the industrial dislocations and short-term unemployment that are alleged to arise from trade liberalization? [Steven] Globerman argues that empirical evidence does not support this contention either. Canadian and American protective tariffs have been reduced over time, yet there has been neither diminution of environmental standards nor enforcement of them. In the EU [European Union], pressure from those countries enforcing the rules and adopting their own tough antipollution laws is apparently bringing about compliance by all members. The bottom line is that each country must decide for itself what the optimal combination of trade and environmental policies suits it best because of differences in preferences, income, and the assimilative capacities of natural resources.

Growth, Trade, and Pollution

Lomborg cites a 1972 World Bank study that investigated whether there is a general tendency for economic growth to lead to lower environmental quality initially, but then later for growth to push in the opposite direction. The study found that in the first phases of growth, countries tend to pollute more, after which their pollution levels fall. Lomborg argues that pollution has fallen for all nations at all levels of wealth and believes that "this is due to continuing technological development, which makes it possible to produce the same amount of goods while imposing less of a burden on the environment. Developing countries can buy progressively cheaper, cleaner technology from the West."

In specific reference to NAFTA, Bruce Yandle observes:

[T]he Office of the U.S. Trade Representative developed a "hit list" of industries vulnerable to the intertwined forces of reduced tariffs and high-cost pollution control. . . . After examining 445 U.S. industries, the analysts found eleven vulnerable to the effects of environmental rules, reduced tariffs, and relaxed investment restrictions. The "hit list" industries are specialty steel, petroleum refining, five categories of chemicals, including medicinal compounds, iron foundries, blast furnaces, and steel mills, explosives, and mineral wool. Probing deeper, the commission's report notes that ten of the eleven industries have high capital intensity, thus reducing the likelihood that plants will relocate to take advantage of lower environmental costs in Mexico. . . . Finally, environmental quality may improve because new plants tend to use the latest technology and equipment, which reduce inefficiencies and pollution.

The main implication of the trade commission's study is that without searching and detailed analysis, industry-by-industry, environmental problems alleged to be the consequence of trade liberalization will likely be grossly exaggerated.

> "Major environmental problems have worsened since trade liberalization began in Mexico."

Free Trade May Lead to More Environmental Harm than Economic Growth

Kevin P. Gallagher

The so-called Environmental Kuznets Curve shows that while environmental damage increases at the beginning of economic development, increasing per-capita income eventually leads to a decrease in environmental damage. However, as Boston University international relations professor Kevin P. Gallagher shows in the following viewpoint, most developing countries' per-capita incomes are far below the turning points. Nor does free trade lead to rapid growth, as the Mexican experience after NAFTA (the North American Free Trade Agreement) shows. These facts account for the worsening environmental situation in Mexico after trade liberalization. Gallagher is a senior researcher at Tufts University's Global Development and Environment Institute and the author of Free Trade and the Environment: Mexico, NAFTA and Beyond.

Kevin P. Gallagher, "Is NAFTA Working for Mexico?" *The Environmental Forum*, May-June 2006. Reproduced by permission.

As you read, consider the following questions:

1. What does Gallagher relate as the lowest estimate of a "turning point" for the Environmental Kuznets Curve? The highest?

2. According to the author, how fast has environmental damage grown compared to income and population growth in Mexico?

3. What percentage of gross domestic product did environmental damage cost Mexico per year between 1988 and 2002, according to Gallagher?

Negotiated in the early 1990s and entering into force in 1994, NAFTA [North America Free Trade Agreement] is a free trade agreement that reduces tariffs and other barriers to trade among the three North American countries. During the NAFTA negotiations, most proponents of the accord argued that free trade would lead to seemingly automatic improvements in environmental conditions in countries like Mexico. Opponents said that the environment would automatically worsen in Mexico, because its lower standards would attract highly polluting firms from the United States—that Mexico would serve as a pollution haven for U.S. industry. Both were wrong.

The Environmental Kuznets Curve

The proponents were generalizing from the so-called Environmental Kuznets Curve [EKC] hypothesis. Among his many contributions, the Nobel Prize–winning economist Simon Kuznets (1901–1985) is well known for two in particular. First, he's the guy who brought us the concept of national accounts—the measurement of GNP [gross national product] and GDP [gross domestic product]. Second, he analyzed the relationship between income growth and inequality, portraying his data in what became known as the Kuznets Curve— the theory that social inequality first increases, then later decreases, as capita income grows over time. Studies in the early 1990s reported a similar relationship between environmental degradation and levels of income: an inverted-U curve showing that environmental degradation may sharply increase in the early stages of economic development, but the rise in per capita income past a certain "turning point" seemed to gradually reduce environmental damage.

Economists hypothesized that environmental decline and then improvement beyond the turning point of the Environmental Kuznets Curve occurs for three reasons. First are so-called scale effects: increases in growth correspond with increases in pollution. However, scale effects can be offset by what are called composition and technique effects. Composition effects occur when economies shift toward services and other less pollution-intensive economic activities. Finally, technique effects occur when increasing income eventually leads to higher levels of environmental awareness, which translates into more stringent environmental policies as the growing middle class demands a cleaner environment.

In 1991 two economists at Princeton University, Gene Grossman and Alan Krueger, examined the relationship between income growth and air pollutants such as sulfur and particulate matter and suggested the turning point at which economies would begin to get less pollution-intensive in these emissions is a per capita income between $3,000 and $5,000 in 1985 Purchasing Power Parity [PPP] dollars.[1] Though the economists were cautious in drawing sweeping conclusions from their research, free trade proponents went wild. Indeed, these findings led to the policy prescription now heard in many negotiating rooms: that the environment can wait, since economic growth will eventually (and naturally) result in environmental improvement.

1. Purchasing Power Parity measures income in terms of what the money will buy in a given country.

Conflicting Real World Evidence

EKC studies have become a cottage industry, with close to 100 scholarly articles published since the original 15 years ago [1991]. What is ironic is the fact that, as the policy community has rushed to push the EKC into the political realm, the consensus in the peer-reviewed economics literature on the EKC has become much more cautious. Most importantly, the literature shows that the empirical evidence for the EKC is relatively weak. The economist David Stern reviewed this literature in a 2004 issue of the journal *World Development* in a paper suitably titled "The Rise and Fall of the Environmental Kuznets Curve."

In Stern's review, too vast to summarize here, two points stand out. First, whereas some air pollutants behave the way the EKC hypothesis would predict, other environmental problems like carbon emissions and deforestation increase in lockstep with income. Second, the EKC turning points are much higher than original estimates. A number of articles have found turning points ranging from $7,500 GDP per capita to $15,000 (in 1985 PPP dollars) and higher. (Please remember these figures are per capita *national* income, not personal income.) What's more, 28 percent of the more than 100 EKC test cases found no turning points, and for those that did find an inverted-U the average turning point was $12,749.

Turning points of $3,000 to $5,000 GDP per capita were conveniently at the world's mean income at the time NAFTA was negotiated, suggesting that a trade pact might just put you over the hump. But the much higher turning points that are more likely to occur imply that pollution per capita (some of it irreversible) may continue for decades before dropping.

Free Trade, Slow Growth, Environmental Damage

Mexico once was the poster child of a closed economy. Dating back to the 1940s, it had high import tariffs to help create do-

Environmental Kuznets Curve for Sulfur Emissions

This graph suggests that, as income increases, emissions decline. The reality in Mexico in recent decades has caused some researchers to question the accuracy of such projections.

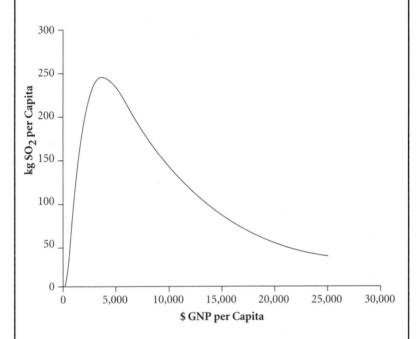

TAKEN FROM: T.Panayotou, *Empirical Tests of Environmental Degradation at Different Stages of Economic Development,* International Labour Office, Geneva, 1993.

mestic industries. Since 1985, however, Mexico has embarked on a series of reforms that have made it one of the most open economies in the world. Mexico reached $5,000 GDP per capita in 1985, precisely the year it began opening its economy. Since then, rises in income have been small and environmental degradation has been large. Statistics from Mexico's National Institute for Statistics, Geography, and Information Systems (whose Mexican acronym is INEGI) document that even though growth has been slow, environmental degradation has been extensive.

First, since 1985 real incomes have grown at approximately 1 percent per capita. But Mexico grew at a rate over 5 percent between 1950 and 1985. To make another comparison, China, with much more restricted markets, has grown at over 7 percent. So, despite massive increases in exports and foreign investment due in part to trade liberalization, such increases have not translated into raising the Mexican standard of living. Clearly, trade liberalization is not a guarantee of growth, and restricted markets like China's can grow at a rapid rate, contrary to the theories of the free trade cognoscenti.

Second, major environmental problems have worsened since trade liberalization began in Mexico. INEGI data covering the period of 1985 to 2002 (the last year of reported data) show that despite the fact that Mexico reached levels of income beyond the range of predicted EKC turning points, national levels of soil erosion, municipal solid waste, and urban air and water pollution have increased faster than both GDP and population growth. (Carbon dioxide emissions per capita have gone down.)

And environmental degradation has been costly to Mexico's prospects for development. The figure given earlier for the financial costs of Mexico's environmental degradation comes from the INEGI study. INEGI estimated that 10 percent of GDP from 1988 to 2002—an average of more than $50 billion per year—went down the drain (or up the stack, etc.). In other words, for every dollar that the Mexican economy grows, 10 cents is thrown away. In effect, environmental degradation is like an additional tax placed on the Mexican people, a tax that gives nothing in return. Wasting $50 billion per year hurts a lot, given that close to half of Mexico's 100 million people live on less than $2 a day.

Harvard University economist Theodore Panayotou has argued that because it may take decades for developing nations like Mexico to reach EKC turning points, the accumulated environmental damages may far exceed the present value of higher future growth. Thus, he says, environmental protection in developing countries may be justified on purely economic grounds.

Trading Growth for Environmental Damage

In my 2004 book *Free Trade and the Environment: Mexico, NAFTA, and Beyond* I evaluated whether Panayotou's hypothesis is justified in the case of air emissions in Mexico. I estimated the number of years it would take for the country to reach EKC turning points of $7,500, $10,000, and $15,000 in 1985 PPP dollars (based on the perhaps lofty assumption that income would grow twice as fast as it did from 1985 to 1999), the amount of environmental damage that would occur at each turning point (based on the pollution growth rate from 1985 to 1999), and the present value of the economic costs of that environmental damage. I based the pollution and economic cost estimates on data from the INEGI report. According to these calculations, it would take Mexico until 2028 to reach $7,500 GDP per capita, 2057 to reach $10,000, and until 2097 to reach $15,000 (all in 1985 PPP dollars). Depending on which discount rate is used for the calculations, the future costs of air pollution damages alone for Mexico could range from $79–270 billion if viewed in present terms—or one fifth to three fifths of Mexico's GDP. These estimates are in no way precise, but they do make the point that Mexico may be trading future growth for environmental degradation.

"Now that several countries in the South
have acquired comparative advantage
in manufactured goods, the North is
hiding behind environmental barriers
to protect their industries."

Protectionist Measures Can Masquerade as Environmental Concerns

Shahrukh Rafi Khan

*Shahrukh Rafi Khan, visiting professor of economics at Mount
Holyoke College in Massachusetts, is the former executive director of the Sustainable Development Policy Institute in Islama-
bad, Pakistan.*

*Taking the viewpoint of a policy maker in a less-developed
country, Khan analyzes theories about the effect of free trade on
the environment that predict that free trade harms the environment in less-developed countries. He states that advanced countries in the Northern Hemisphere could use these concerns to
avoid opening up their markets to goods produced in the poorer
southern countries. Khan reviews several studies that deal with
these issues and concludes that in general these types of environ-*

Shahrukh Rafi Khan, *Trade and Environment: Difficult Policy Choices at the Interface*,
London: Zed Books, 2002, pp. 17–22. Copyright © 2002 Shahrukh Rafi Khan. Reproduced by permission.

mental harm are not as significant as predicted and that trade can actually promote better environmental regulations in the global South. He contends that industrializing countries should comply with northern environmental concerns, despite their costs.

As you read, consider the following questions:

1. According to the author, how much, as a percentage of total costs, are the average costs for U.S. industries of complying with environmental regulations?

2. With regard to the agricultural sector, what did economists discover about the relationship between trade openness and the strictness of environmental regulations, as noted by Khan?

3. Why does the author believe that, despite their costs, less-developed countries should comply with advanced countries' environmental requirements for trade?

The poor Southern countries are currently in a double bind. On the one hand, they find that the rich countries are being very slow in implementing the Uruguay Round trade agreements [implemented in 1994] in liberalizing imports, particularly in sectors of interest to them, such as textiles and agriculture. On the other hand, the world trade scenario is changing, independently of the sway of the WTO [World Trade Organization], as governments and businesses respond to consumer preferences for ecologically friendly production and consumption and set and impose environmental standards. Thus even the goods currently being exported are increasingly being expected to meet stringent environmental standards.

Poor countries now feel that when it suited the North, they preached consumer sovereignty and confronted them with the 'let the market decide' rhetoric. Now that several countries in the South have acquired comparative advantage in manufactured goods, the North is hiding behind environmental barriers to protect their industries, and setting aside the market ideology they preached.

The issue is not quite as simple as it seems. If standards are responding to consumer preferences in the North, then the market ideology still prevails, and Northern consumers in effect choose to consume goods that are produced by cleaner methods rather than those that are cheaper. However, Southern countries may need to be wary of the protectionist use of environmental standards by rich country governments rather than those dictated by the market. In such cases, they should lobby via the WTO to ensure that the old-time market rule of consumers' sovereignty prevails, particularly now that this benefits the poor countries. . . .

Social Costs and Trade

Traditional trade theory, based on the concept of 'comparative advantage', claims that trade brings mutual benefits to all parties engaged in exchange. However, the theory of comparative advantage assumes that all external costs are internalized, when typically they are not. The terms of trade of a country thus do not reflect the social costs involved in the production and consumption of goods and services to be traded.

The trade and environment literature deals with a number of other issues and hypotheses that are not a part of traditional trade theory. Many of these are related to concerns in the North or the South about fair trade. First, that trade liberalization could result in strategic movement on the part of Northern multinational corporations to Southern countries with more lax environmental regulations and hence result in a loss in Northern jobs. Second, that the North could use trade liberalization to dump its dirty technology and other domestically prohibited goods (DPGs) on the South. Third, that the structural adjustment induced export promotion could result in the South exporting its environmental capital in the form of high domestic pollution and resource degradation. Fourth, that the multilateral environmental agreements (MEAs) are increasingly affecting the world trading environment and these MEAs could block Southern exports. Fifth, that the North has a greater resource and technological ability to meet the standards it sets and that this will mean blocking access to Southern exports and enhancing its market share. Sixth, that the cost of mitigating such pollution in the South is very high. The literature on these issues is reviewed in greater detail in the next section.

Avoiding Pollution Regulations

Companies in the North may fear that, with the dismantling of trade barriers, developing countries may have a competitive edge due to their less stringent or more lax enforcement of environmental regulations. This might lead to a relocation of factories to developing countries to take advantage of lax environmental regulations and/or enforcement. [Environmental economists Robert] Repetto, [Judith M.] Dean and [James] Tobey refute this hypothesis. They argue that relocating a plant entails complex and lengthy processes, which include selling an existing plant, severing its workforce, relocation of key personnel, choosing a new site, building a new factory, and recruiting and training new staff. All these processes are not feasible just to take advantage of savings on pollution control cost that total less than 2 percent of total sales. The *World Development Report* also states that environmental costs are a minor share of output value—averaging only 0.5 per cent for all US industries in 1988 and 3 per cent for the most polluting industry.

[Economists Muthu Kumara] Mani and [David] Wheeler find, using cross-country analysis, that the evidence seems consistent with the pollution haven pattern of investment. However, upon closer examination, they suggest that there are several other reasons explaining 'dirty production' in the South that have little to do with the 'pollution haven' story.

Imports of Dirty Industry into the South

Developing countries feel threatened that, with trade liberalization (that is, reduced tariffs on imported capital and intermediate goods), there may be an influx of dirty technology coming into their countries. While evidence on this is limited, there was an instance in Pakistan in which a second-hand Danish mercury chlor-alkali plant was being imported in 1994. Greenpeace International, with the support of local environmental organizations, frustrated this attempt. Similarly, the newspapers reported on the proposed dumping of toxic wastes off the coast of Pakistan's Balochistan province. Thus the world environmental community needs to be alert to the disposal of various DPGs including 'dirty machinery', toxic wastes, insecticides, fertilizers, chemicals and pharmaceuticals.

Over-harvesting and Environmental Damage

Critics of the free trade ideology claim that increased exports, particularly in the aftermath of liberalization, will be at the cost of natural resource depletion and degradation and increased industrial pollution. Thus the World Commission on Environment and Development pointed out, in what is referred to as the Brundtland Report, that, during the 1980s, the South's commodity trade was based on the over-harvesting of nature in order to service its debt. The problem is especially acute in that the South lacks the resources and technological prowess to combat environmental degradation.

Proponents of liberalization argue that, quite to the contrary, enhanced exports are likely to benefit the environment in the long run. [N.] Birdsall and [D.] Wheeler point out that competition will induce the drive toward the latest manufacturing technologies and that, since these are likely to be pro-

"Green" Campaigns Mask Protectionism

All over Europe, . . . home-grown campaigns are being promoted, attacking Africa's newest and most successful export products. . . .

African success stories are threatened by this new 'stay local' trend. . . .

None of the few African countries that have managed to enter European markets with agricultural products that compete with local producers have had an easy path reaching their position. Food quality and hygiene standards in Europe are extremely rigid and to a large degree designed to exclude foreign competition. To be able to reach sceptical European consumers, African producers mostly also have been obliged to follow strict environmental and social guidelines.

Also, African food products for years had to fight against false prototypes promoted by seemingly well-meaning antiglobalisation activists that to a great degree were funded by local farmer organisations. Development specialists—who do not get much air-time in European media—had to explain on and on again that European consumers were not "stealing food from starving Africans' when buying their products, but that these imports indeed would promote wealth and empowerment in rural Africa.

Rainer Hennig, Afrol News, www.afrol.com.

cured from the North, they are likely to be much cleaner. Further, Northern importers may require cleaner processes to ensure greener products. They present evidence from their own cross-country analysis showing greater openness to be associated with less pollution-intensive industrialization. [P.] Eliste and [Per G.] Fredriksson (1998) find that, for the agricultural sector, trade liberalization does not induce a 'race to the bottom'. Their findings suggest a positive relationship between stringency of environmental regulations and trade openness. Their findings also suggest that there is a positive association of the degree of stringency in regulations among trading partners. . . .

Multinational Trade Agreements and Environmental Protection

In recent years, trade policy has been considered as an instrument to enforce environmental compliance in the form of inclusion of trade provisions in MEAs. These may include unilateral use of trade measures to enforce environmental compliance on the part of trading partners. The sanctions, if applied, would mean that trade with non-parties to the agreement would in principle be prohibited. So far the WTO has not endorsed the use of such sanctions. Nevertheless, these MEAs are an important feature in the trade-environment interface.

The provisions of the Montreal Protocol required signatories to ban imports of CFCs (chlorofluorocarbons) and products containing CFCs from non-signatory countries. Precedence now exists regarding the unilateral use of trade measures to enforce environmental compliance—the US ban on shrimp imports to encourage the use of turtle-excluder devices to protect sea turtles is a case in point. The Convention on International Trade in Endangered Species (CITES) has agreed to a ban on ivory. Other countries have import bans on whales, fur seals, polar bears and some specific migratory birds and species. The Basle Convention bans some types of trade in hazardous and toxic wastes.

Meeting Environmental Standards

The emphasis by the Northern environmental community on uniformity of production and process methods and environmental effects of production processes is interpreted by the

South as an effort to restrict its access to Northern markets. The argument is that Southern countries do not have the capacity of Northern countries to cope with detailed regulation, and also that the regulations are tailored to Northern concerns and may thus be inappropriate. Thus any benefits of liberalization and environmental conservation, in the presence of harmonized standards, will be skewed in favour of the North. Brazil raised this issue originally in 1993 over European Union regulations for tissue paper production. Brazilian pulp manufacturers complained that the regulations on consumption of renewable and non-renewable resources, waste generation and sulphur emissions would disadvantage foreign producers who could not meet these standards. [Economist Atul] Kaushik reviews various cases for India and finds that the high standards are so rigorous in some cases that they could be viewed as protectionist. Further, sometimes they may be motivated by Northern producers wanting to market alternatives. Not only in the case of compliance are costs prohibitive, but legitimate questions regarding environmental justification can be raised and there is often an irrelevance of Northern standards. Finally, there is a lack of concession to local Southern conditions, such as the supply of sustainably produced wood in the supplier's market.

Environmental Protection Worth the Costs

Many Southern countries exporting to the OECD [Organization for Economic Cooperation and Development] countries have had to confront standards, particularly in the leather and textile industries, and this is viewed as an unfair protectionist cost being imposed on them by Northern governments. Our take on this issue differs. Southern countries such as Pakistan must distinguish between restrictions imposed by Northern governments and those imposed by Northern businesses. If Northern governments impose import restrictions because Southern countries are not doing enough about child labour or cleaning up production technologies, this constitutes a non-tariff barrier. However, this is not the big danger that faces Southern exporters. Increasingly, businesses in the North are being required by their boards/shareholders to do business with firms that meet certain 'voluntary' environmental and quality standards. In some ways, a cleaner environment is viewed as a luxury good and the more prosperous Northern consumers are viewed as requiring it. This is thus a market-dictated standard and not as such a non-tariff barrier imposed by Northern governments. This is a very important distinction. The only option Southern exporters have is to conform or lose markets.

Even if Northern governments impose standards and they provide an edge to Northern producers who are more capable of meeting them, it would still be wise for LDCs [least developed countries] to conform. Various product-related environmental standards should be seen as an ongoing consumer protection movement in the North. While various process-related standards can legitimately be viewed as impediments to trade, as long as governments impose these, it is difficult to argue with consumer sovereignty in the North. Further, . . . our view is that cleaning up production processes generates far more social benefits than costs in producer countries, and wins markets as well.

"The facts simply do not support claims that international competition leads exporters to reduce wages. . . . The opposite is the case."

Free Trade Improves Labor Conditions

Robert J. Flanagan

Robert J. Flanagan is the Konosuke Matsushita Professor of International Labor Economics and Policy Analysis at the Stanford Graduate School of Business. He is the author of Labor Economics and Labor Relations *as well as* Globalization and Labor Conditions: Working Conditions and Worker Rights in a Global Economy, *from which the following viewpoint is taken.*

In the viewpoint, Flanagan makes the case that free trade helps workers by increasing demand for labor. The more companies operating in less-developed countries produce for the export market, the more labor is required, he contends. Eventually labor shortages result, and companies are forced to raise wages to attract workers, he concludes. Flanagan asserts that this process is already happening in China, despite its massive numbers of available workers.

As you read, consider the following questions:

1. In what way can workers "vote" in nondemocratic China in order to improve their conditions, according to Flanagan?
2. What does the author say is an "export wage premium"?
3. According to Flanagan, how much are the export wage premiums in Korea? In Mexico? In Taiwan?

Does the growth associated with trade liberalization improve or degrade labor conditions relative to growth from domestic sources? Answering this question requires consideration of how export and import growth influence domestic labor conditions. Reducing trade barriers should increase imports of goods and services that are produced more efficiently abroad and increase exports of goods and services that are produced more efficiently at home. . . . A shift of labor from low-productivity, import-competing domestic industries to high-productivity export industries should improve wages and working conditions. The question of how trade expansion alters conditions *within* the export and import-competing sectors requires more investigation, however.

Exports Improve Labor Conditions

The claim that free trade degrades labor conditions is hardest to understand when open trade policies increase foreign demand for a country's exports and for the services of workers to produce those exports. What then happens to wages and other working conditions depends entirely on labor supply conditions, which themselves are determined by the labor market alternatives available to workers. Much the same may be said of the additional demand for labor from foreign direct investment in a country.

For economies with substantial unemployment or underemployment, the availability of new jobs in the export sector will be enough to attract additional workers. Improvements in working conditions will not be necessary. Such "perfectly elastic" supply conditions in which companies can hire as many workers as they wish at the existing wage are likely to be the norm in countries with huge reserves of underemployed rural agricultural labor or very high urban unemployment rates. Increased export demand is unlikely to improve working conditions in such countries until the reserves of labor are employed. But the additional job opportunities provided by increased export demand will raise total wage income and should not degrade further the working conditions established in the face of significant unemployment. In many countries the floor under working conditions may be a "social minimum" set by public policies.

For economies that are approximately fully employed, firms that produce exports will have to meet increased export demand by attracting workers away from other jobs. To do so, export firms will have to offer wages and working conditions that are superior to what workers already earn in agriculture, in the informal sector, or at other companies in the formal sector. Employers in the latter sectors may raise wages and improve other working conditions in an effort to retain workers in the face of job offers from export firms. Either way, working conditions will improve.

The Case of China

No country illustrates these mechanisms as clearly as modern China, a country long regarded as a bastion of cheap labor. By 2005, a *New York Times* report would note that China, "which has powered its stunning economic rise with a cheap and supposedly bottomless pool of migrant labor, is experiencing shortages of about two million workers in Guangdong and Fujian, the two provinces at the heart of China's export-driven economy." By 2004, two decades of strict family planning policies that limited families to one child was showing up as reduced labor flows from rural to urban manufacturing areas.

Employment in Export Processing Zones, 2002

Region	Number of zones	Employment in zones (000s)
Asia	749	36,824
Central America and Mexico	3,300	2,242
Middle East	37	691
North Africa	23	441
Sub-Saharan Africa	64	431
North America	713	330
South America	39	311
Transition economies	90	246
Caribbean	87	226
Europe	55	51
Other	17	141
TOTAL	5,174	41,934

TAKEN FROM: Robert J. Flanagan, *Globalization and Labor Conditions: Working Conditions and Worker Rights in a Global Economy*. Oxford: Oxford University Press, 2006.

At the same time, export demand for Chinese products continued to grow. As a result, "young migrant workers coveted by factories are gaining bargaining power and many are choosing to leave the low pay and often miserable conditions in Guangdong. In nondemocratic China, it is the equivalent of 'voting with their feet.'" The stronger labor market conditions serve two functions. Working conditions improve for Chinese workers who now have more job vacancies to choose from and can leave employers offering inferior conditions. Such employers must improve wages and other working conditions in order to recruit workers. In addition, some of the benefits of a tighter Chinese labor market spread to other low-wage countries, such as Vietnam, Cambodia, and India as some companies try to escape higher labor costs in China. Some

Chinese manufacturers "could face a fate familiar to many manufacturers in the United States—they would have to move to a country with cheaper workers." The additional demand raises employment and eventually wages in other low-wage countries.

Conceptually, export producers could force wages down in only two cases. The first seems rather special and unlikely: increased export production would force pay down if it increased monopsony power—that is, if it reduced workers' choice of employers by increasing employer concentration. But it is hard to see how increased export production would increase employer concentration. In countries with elastic labor supply, the social minimum or work in agriculture or informal sectors limit monopsony power. More important, the Internet enables workers in even the poorest countries to stay more informed about employment alternatives than ever before. Workers who might have known only of local employment options in the past can now easily compare their current job conditions to job opportunities available in other cities and regions. The second case is more plausible: some governments may suspend labor regulations and union organizing rights for export producers or in export processing zones (EPZs). Other countries may not enforce labor regulations that apply to exporters. Some examples of such government actions are quite visible. . . . For now, we note that EPZs typically account for a small fraction of national employment, and the ability of exporters to profit from lax rules depends on working conditions available outside EPZs.

Export Industries Pay Better

Globalization skeptics assume that would-be exporters respond to competitive pressures by cutting labor costs—a response that degrades labor conditions. As we have seen, however, labor supply limits what exporters can do, and supply is determined by the alternatives available to workers. Conditions in export firms may not be attractive from the perspective of industrialized countries, but they are unlikely to be worse than conditions elsewhere in the country. The cure is to provide workers with more, not fewer, alternatives.

Comparisons of wages in export and nonexport firms now exist for both developing countries (Chile, Colombia, Estonia, Korea, Mexico, Taiwan, and sub-Saharan Africa) and some industrialized countries (Germany, Spain, Sweden, and the United States). These studies invariably find that exporters pay higher wages than nonexporters. Moreover, the "export wage premia" are considerably *larger* in less developed countries than in industrialized countries. At one extreme, a study of more than 4,000 manufacturing plants in one German region finds an export wage premium of about 2.6 percent, largely reflecting a premium for white-collar workers. These are the smallest margins found in any of the early studies. Studies of U.S. manufacturing plants find somewhat higher wage premiums, generally in the mid-single digits. Both production and nonproduction workers receive higher wages from exporters. For the European Union, the average wage in export sectors is 109 percent of the average wage in manufacturing.

The export wage premiums in most developing countries seem very large in contrast. Studies of manufacturing plants report export wage premiums of 10–12 percent in Korea, 7–9 percent in Mexico, 15–17 percent in Taiwan and as high as 40 percent in sub-Saharan Africa. The facts simply do not support claims that international competition leads exporters to reduce wages below national norms. Particularly for the poorest countries, the opposite is the case.

> *"By setting a floor for the region's social and environmental policies, the EU (European Union) has tried to encourage a high-road path to development."*

Free-Trade Policies Can Also Protect Human Rights and the Environment

Sarah Anderson and John Cavanagh

Sarah Anderson is the director of the Global Economy Project at the Institute for Policy Studies, a progressive think tank in Washington, DC, and John Cavanagh is director of the institute. In the following viewpoint, they present the EU as a model of achieving closer economic integration among countries without the negative consequences of most free-trade agreements, such as human rights violations and environmental degradation. While the United States has pursued projects like the Free Trade Area of the Americas (FTAA), they argue, the EU has engaged in a more comprehensive approach to economic integration by devoting financial resources to reducing inequality among European countries.

Sarah Anderson and John Cavanagh, "After the FTAA: Lessons from Europe for the Americas," Institute for Policy Studies, June 2005, pp. 2–9. Reproduced by permission.

As you read, consider the following questions:

1. How has the European Union approached the problem of economic inequalities among its member nations, according to Anderson and Cavanagh?
2. What group has traditionally faced discrimination in Europe, in the authors' opinion?
3. Name at least four of the rights guaranteed to workers under the EU's Charter of Fundamental Rights, as reported by Anderson and Cavanagh.

The European Union [EU] is a unique experiment in a broad approach to integration that has attempted to reduce economic and social disparities between rich and poor countries and within member nations. In many ways, it stands in stark contrast to the narrow approach advocated by the U.S. government through deals like the North American Free Trade Agreement [NAFTA].

The idea that the EU offers useful lessons for the Americas has gained support among leaders in the Americas. Mexico's [former president] Vicente Fox has long promoted development funds similar to the EU's structural funds as a way to level the economic playing field in the Americas. Similarly, Argentine president Nestor Kirchner has said that the EU could "find its future because it showed a lot of solidarity towards those who were weaker. . . . Otherwise, you just deepen asymmetries." . . .

The European Union treaty states that "the community shall aim at reducing disparities between the levels of development of the various regions and the backwardness of the least favored regions and islands, including rural areas." Since the early 1960s, the EU has pursued this goal by investing more than $325 billion in grants to poorer countries and poorer regions within richer countries for infrastructure, training, and other development projects. This is roughly ten times the amount of U.S. economic assistance grants to all of Latin

America during this time period. To qualify, national EU governments develop proposals for using the grants in consultation with the European Commission and commit to providing a certain level of co-financing.

Reducing Inequality in Europe

Although the focus today [in 2005] is primarily on the 10 nations that joined the EU in May 2004, the largest recipients of these grants in the past were the former so-called "poor four"—Ireland, Greece, Spain and Portugal. To varying degrees, all have made progress in catching up with the other EU member states. Indeed, Ireland has become one of the wealthiest countries in the world. Between 1982 and 2003, Spain and Portugal increased their GDP [gross domestic product] per capita levels from 74 to 83 and 61 to 69 percent of the EU average, respectively. Greece did less well in the 1980s, but has caught up by 10 percentage points since an infusion of aid in the 1990s. Moreover, the European Commission claims that these funds maintained or created 2.2 million jobs in these countries during this period.

By contrast, the proposed FTAA [Free Trade Area of the Americas] contained no mechanisms to reduce inequalities. Based on the model of the North American Free Trade Agreement (NAFTA), the assumption was that trade and investment liberalization alone would be enough to raise standards in North America's "poor one"—Mexico. The deal did result in large increases in exports and foreign investment, but this did not translate into increased prosperity. Mexico has fallen further behind in per capita income as a percentage of the North American average. This figure was 43 percent in 1982, 33 at the start of NAFTA [1994], and 30 in 2003.

The EU's development grants have also paid off for the richer countries that are the primary contributors. The European Commission estimates that about 25 percent of grants have returned to the higher-income countries in the EU in the form of increased imports, especially machinery and equipment.

Possibilities for the Americas

The general lesson from the EU experience is that trade and investment liberalization are no guarantee of better living standards. Resource transfer is necessary to allow cash-strapped governments to invest in the infrastructure and human resources that are crucial to long-term prosperity. Easing the financial strain in impoverished countries also benefits people in the richer nations. First, it would likely make developing countries stronger trading partners. Secondly, it would relieve some of the pressure that many developing country governments face to attract foreign investment by offering an exploited workforce and lax environmental enforcement, practices which undermine efforts to maintain high standards in the North.

Nevertheless, there are considerable doubts over whether EU-style development grants could ever be applied in the Western Hemisphere. While Canada gives a relatively large percent of its GDP toward development assistance, the United States does not; it routinely ranks last in this category among wealthy countries. Many have also pointed out that there are limits to the levels of support that the richer Western European countries are willing to commit. The 10 new EU member states are not receiving the same level of support enjoyed in the past by Ireland, Portugal, Greece, and Spain. How then could we ever imagine such large sums committed to the even poorer countries in the Western Hemisphere?

Rather than attempting to duplicate the European model, the challenge is to think creatively about the forms of resource transfer that would be feasible and appropriate for this region. A rich discussion around innovative methods of generating development funds is taking place in the context of the Millennium Development Goals (MDG) launched by the United Nations in 2000. Governments and international financial institutions have committed to trying to achieve these goals by 2015, including the objective of cutting world poverty in half. Many of the ideas being discussed for financing the MDGs could also be incorporated into a new type of hemispheric agreement in the Americas. . . .

Anti-discrimination Policies

The EU requires member states to comply with high standards on labor rights, gender equity, racial discrimination, health and safety, environment and other issues. By setting a floor for the region's social and environmental policies, the EU has tried to encourage a high-road path to development, instead of competition based on exploitation in areas of weak standards.

The EU's social standards have evolved and expanded over the years. In 2000, they consolidated the whole range of civil, political, economic and social rights into one text, the European Union Charter of Fundamental Rights. While the Charter itself has not been legally binding, parts of it are the basis for EU directives, regulations, and decisions that must be transposed into national legislation. And soon the full charter may become legally binding, since it is included in a proposed EU Constitution now being considered in national referenda. [The EU constitution was tabled after French and Dutch citizens voted against it in 2005.]

The EU has taken a particularly strong stance in defending women's rights. In the 1970s, regulations established requirements for equal treatment for men and women in employment and training. Directives in the 1980s and early 1990s dealt with equal treatment in social security and protections for pregnant workers. The Irish government tried to negotiate a waiver from the pay equity directive, but the request was refused. Likewise in Austria, it was only when the EU issued a directive on parental leave that Austrian unions won a long-standing battle to obtain that right.

In addition to the progress on women's issues, there is considerable optimism that two relatively new directives will have a positive impact in the broader area of discrimination. Adopted in 2000, these directives cover sex, disability, religion or belief, sexual orientation, age, and racial or ethnic origin. One is known as the Race Directive and provides protection in education, social security, access to goods and services, and cultural life. The other is the Employment Directive, which covers employment, self-employment, working conditions, membership in workers' organizations, and whistle-blowing. One way in which EU anti-discrimination standards are having an impact is in addressing long-standing problems of racism against the Roma (sometimes referred to as Gypsies), Europe's largest ethnic minority. In the new member state of Slovakia, for example, the EU has pressured the government to adopt anti-discrimination laws to protect the Roma from common abuses, such as the practice of wrongly placing Roma children in schools for the disabled.

Labor Rights

The Charter on Fundamental Rights includes extensive protections for workers and trade unions. They encompass:

- The right to basic social security

- The right to vocational and further training

- The right to a written labor contract

- Protection against unjustified dismissal

- The right to adequate working conditions

- The right to health and safety protection in the workplace

- The right to limited working hours

- The right to paid vacation

- The right to equality between EU aliens and EU citizens

- The right to information and consultation in the company

- The right to free and independent trade unions

- The right to collective bargaining

On some more controversial matters, the EU thus far has chosen not to take action, for example on minimum wage levels and the right to strike. These matters are left in the hands of national governments.

Environmental Protection

EU regulations also cover a wide range of environmental issues, including water quality standards, nature conservation, waste management, climate change, industrial accidents, nuclear safety and radiation protection, and protection of coastal and urban areas. Environmental impact assessments are also required on all relevant EU policies.

Critics charge that enforcement is constrained by the fact that the European Commission must rely on national-level environmental reporting systems, which are lacking in many countries. Nevertheless, there are examples of EU environmental laws that have had significant impact. For example, a directive on large combustion plants sets emissions limits that are more easily attained with cleaner natural gas technologies. This law is cited as at least partly responsible for a reduction of energy-related emissions in the energy supply and industry sectors of 43 and 23 percent, respectively, during the past decade. The European Commission also points to a law on urban wastewater that has resulted in a significant decrease in

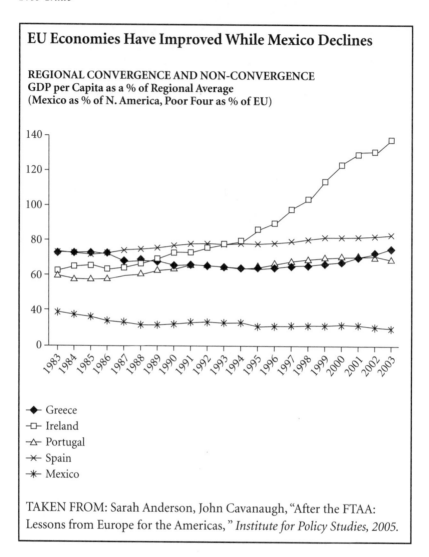

EU Economies Have Improved While Mexico Declines

REGIONAL CONVERGENCE AND NON-CONVERGENCE
GDP per Capita as a % of Regional Average
(Mexico as % of N. America, Poor Four as % of EU)

- ◆ Greece
- -□- Ireland
- -△- Portugal
- -✕- Spain
- -✳- Mexico

TAKEN FROM: Sarah Anderson, John Cavanaugh, "After the FTAA: Lessons from Europe for the Americas," *Institute for Policy Studies, 2005.*

the number of heavily polluted rivers. Organic matter discharges fell by 50 to 80 percent over the last 15 years.

Environmentalists are particularly hopeful about two new regulations to reduce toxic hazards. . . . One will require electronics manufacturers to take back and recycle their products and the other will require manufacturers to eliminate a number of highly toxic substances from all new equipment.

Enforcing Standards

The EU experience with enforcing basic social and environmental standards offers a number of lessons for the Americas. Many developing country leaders and civil society representatives have justifiable concerns that any enforcement mechanism would be manipulated by the richer countries, especially the United States, for narrow protectionist purposes.

The EU has attempted to ameliorate such concerns in at least three ways. One is by emphasizing compliance, rather than punishment, and offering poorer countries considerable financial and technical support to help them achieve the required standards. The second is that the authorities responsible for monitoring and adjudication, the European Commission and the European Court of Justice, are supranational, which helps to distance them from narrow national or political interests. And finally, governments accused of noncompliance are given generous (some say overly generous) amounts of time to correct problems. It is the rare case that reaches the point where the European Court of Justice imposes sanctions, which can range from fines to the ultimate punishment of EU expulsion.

Learning from the European Example

Perhaps the most important general lesson from the EU experience with social and environmental standards is that these regulations are vital, but insufficient to significantly improve living and working conditions in poor countries. Strong regulations are most effective when they are complemented by financial support and other assistance necessary for compliance. This concept has been largely absent from the debate over integration in the Americas. In the United States, a growing number of elected leaders, including seven of the eight men who ran for the Democratic nomination for president in 2004, support the position that labor and environmental provisions should be included in trade agreements. While the recognition that trade has social and environmental impacts is important, a far broader response is necessary to address concerns about the U.S. government's approach to trade policy.

Another important lesson from Europe is that there are ways to design a process for enforcement that includes some positive incentives for compliance and is largely insulated from manipulation by the more powerful countries. While it may not make sense to duplicate the European approach in the Americas, it is an important example of national governments accepting some limitations on their sovereignty in certain areas for the purpose of promoting broader social and environmental goals. Government leaders and civil society representatives in the Americas should engage in a dialogue over how we could best design mechanisms for lifting up social and environmental standards in our region. As in Europe, an important part of the process would be identifying the specific social and environmental issues in our region that would benefit from being addressed at the supranational level.

> "It's quite clear that globalization as we
> know it was never about lifting anyone
> out of poverty; it was about corporate
> profit."

Global Trade Is
Impoverishing Both U.S. and
Developing-World Workers

Jim Goodman

*Jim Goodman is an organic dairy farmer and writer from Wone-
woc, Wisconsin, whose work is online at Counterpunch.org and
Familyfarmdefenders.org. In the following viewpoint, Goodman
holds that more than a decade of free-trade policies has resulted
in the disappearance of high-wage jobs in developed countries,
while in the developing world extreme poverty is still widespread. Building on the ideas of economist Joseph Stiglitz, Goodman makes the case that true development involves a measure of
equality, the improvement of education and health care, and a
degree of control over their own destiny for workers and farmers.*

As you read, consider the following questions:

1. What did advocates of free trade believe would happen
   as trade barriers and tariffs were reduced around the
   world?

Jim Goodman, "Round Up the Usual Experts: Make Them Live on 50 Cents a Day,"
counterpunch.org, January 20, 2007. Reproduced by permission of the author.

161

2. According to Goodman, how are modern corporate leaders like the imperialists of the nineteenth century?

3. What are some of Goodman's suggestions for making global trade more equitable for people in both developed and developing countries?

Perhaps you have noticed? Lots of US auto workers lost their jobs in 2006, lots of workers in other industries as well, farmers, well we don't expect much anymore and even high-tech workers are feeling the pinch. The minimum wage hasn't gone up since 1997 and according to the US Bureau of Labor Statistics, there are currently [as of 2007] 6.8 million unemployed (over 8 million if you count those who have given up trying to find a job). Am I missing something here? I thought that globalization and the founding of the World Trade Organization (WTO) in 1995 was supposed to raise everyone's ship. Instead it seems most of us are losing ground.

Loss of Manufacturing Jobs

Auto manufacturing, or more correctly US manufacturing in general, is steadily outsourcing to countries with large, low-wage work forces, weak environmental standards and dismal worker safety protections; this is globalization. A job on the assembly line at Ford or GM [General Motors] used to mean a secure future with good pay and benefits, now the pink slip could come at any time.

It wasn't supposed to be this way; advocates of the new globalized economy promised as the economies of the developing world grew they would buy even more US-made products (especially after the WTO eradicated tariffs and trade barriers) and everyone's income would rise. But instead of sending them cars, we sent them the jobs—they worked cheaper.

Even Henry Ford, a guy who loved a good profit margin, knew he had to pay his workers wages that enabled them to buy the products they were producing. That thinking seems to have been trampled by the globalization bandwagon. Wages stagnate, benefits are cut, blue collar workers and farmers are forced to join the unemployed to collect food stamps.

While globalization has inflicted job loss, poverty and loss of self-respect on US workers, its effects on the people in developing countries has, in many cases, been even more devastating. According to Joseph Stiglitz, winner of the Nobel Prize in economics and former chief economist of the World Bank, the number of people living in poverty has increased by almost 100 million over the last decade. This occurred while world income increased an average of 2.5 percent!

Growing Division Between Rich and Poor

And still, the division between the rich and the poor continues to grow. An estimated 1 billion people live on less than a dollar a day, half of the world's population on less than two dollars, while the corporations, the chief proponents and beneficiaries of globalization, continue to push for even more trade liberalization and the opening of developing economies to foreign investment. Isn't this a bit absurd, or criminal? While 1 billion people live on less than a dollar a day and the promise of poverty reduction has utterly failed, the captains of industry and investment who championed globalization are rewarded for their promotion of world poverty with multimillion-dollar bonuses.

Much like the colonial empires of Europe who sought natural riches and the indigenous labor to extract it from their colonies, today's corporate globalizers seek that same cheap labor, those same natural resources and the support and protection of their industrialized governments and financial institutions.

It's quite clear that globalization as we know it was never about lifting anyone out of poverty; it was about corporate profit. While world trade has helped many countries lift their standard of living, that was the case only if the course of development and economic growth was determined by those countries—not corporations, not the industrialized countries of the North, and certainly not the International Monetary Fund (IMF).

Trade Liberalization Benefits

Stiglitz is highly critical of rapid trade liberalization that is forced upon developing countries by international economic institutions that are dominated by wealthy industrialized nations and the commercial and financial interests in those countries. "They are not representative of the nations they serve." Forcing developing countries to open their economies to foreign competition before they are fully ready to do so is a recipe for disaster. "Jobs have systematically been destroyed— poor farmers in developing countries simply couldn't compete with the highly subsidized goods from Europe and America. IMF policies in developing countries have led to interest rates that would make job creation impossible, even in the best of circumstances. Since no safety nets were in place, those that lost their jobs were forced into poverty."

Muhammad Yunis, winner of the Nobel Peace Prize [in] 2006, also criticized globalization as being a profit-driven force that unfairly benefited the rich and powerful at the expense of the poor. Globalization can bring benefits to the poor, but to do so it must have rules, [Yunis states,] "rules that ensure that the poorest have a place and piece of the action, without being elbowed out by the strong. Globalization must not become financial imperialism."

Well, that is exactly what it has become, that was the intent of the neo-conservative movement all along. Because the rich apparently know how to handle money and the poor don't, are we supposed to finalize this class division thing and impoverish everyone for the benefit of the top one or two percent?

Globalization Must Be Reshaped

Today, with the continuing decline in transportation and communication costs, and the reduction of man-made barriers to the flow of goods, services, and capital (though there remain serious barriers to the free flow of labor), we have a process of "globalization" analogous to the earlier processes in which national economies were formed. Unfortunately, we have no world government, accountable to the people of every country, to oversee the globalization process in a fashion comparable to the way national governments guided the nationalization process. Instead, we have a system that might be called *global governance without global government*, one in which a few institutions—the World Bank, the IMF, the WTO—and a few players—the finance, commerce, and trade ministries, closely linked to certain financial and commercial interests—dominate the scene, but in which many of those affected by their decisions are left almost voiceless. It's time to change some of the rules governing the international economic order, to think once again about how decisions get made at the international level—and in whose interests—and to place less emphasis on ideology and to look more at what works. It is crucial that the successful development we have seen in East Asia be achieved elsewhere. There is an enormous cost to continuing global instability. Globalization can be reshaped, and when it is, when it is properly, fairly run, with all countries having a voice in policies affecting them, there is a possibility that it will help create a new global economy in which growth is not only more sustainable and less volatile but the fruits of this growth are more equitably shared.

Joseph E. Stiglitz,
Globalization and Its Discontents, *2002.*

A Spiral to the Bottom

Globalization needs rules, strong rules. Here in the United States, we assume everyone wants to be like us; well, they don't. They may want some of the economic security and safety nets we and other industrialized countries have, but plopping a few Kentucky Fried Chicken franchises down here and there in developing countries, or making sure stores have Levis and Nikes on their shelves does not mean globalization is working or those countries have pulled themselves out of poverty. Consumerism is not a measure of success just because we say it is; our consumer society has more than its share of economic inequality.

Global trade agreements must provide for a living wage and social justice for workers. So far it has been little more than a spiral to the bottom, pulling wages down to the lowest level. Life, liberty and the pursuit of happiness, denied to the sweatshop workers and poor of the world, and perhaps only a memory to all but America's elite.

Environmental protection and worker safety cannot be compromised. Developing countries are not "throw away societies." They cannot be used as toxic waste dumps for our outdated consumer goods, nor can their farmers and workers be expected to use chemicals banned in the industrialized world.

The Right to Choose

We must let the developing world make their own choices based on their culture and the political process they aspire to. They should not be forced to accept development plans based on the economic wishes of the industrialized world and its economic institutions.

Food is a basic human right. The food sovereignty of developing nations cannot be compromised by the subsidized agriculture of industrialized nations; furthermore, food has no place in international trade agreements. All nations have a right to decide what they will eat, how it will be grown and who will control it. No one should be allowed to patent indigenous people, plants or animals, or force them to accept seed or food they do not want.

Having viewed globalization from the top, Joseph Stiglitz perhaps says it best, "Development is about transforming societies, improving the lives of the poor, enabling everyone to have a chance at success and access to health care and education."

We have a responsibility to make new rules for globalization; we owe it to ourselves, the workers and the poor of the industrialized world, but perhaps more so to the poor of the developing world. They have been exploited long enough.

Periodical Bibliography

The following articles have been selected to supplement the diverse views presented in this chapter.

| Mark Engler and Nadia Martinez | "Oiled Again: Free Trade Agreement Threatens Costa Rican Environmental Protections," *Grist: Environmental News and Commentary*, March 26, 2004. |

Yves Engler — "The Case for Protectionism," *Ecologist*, December 2003.

Jeffrey Frankel — "Climate and Trade," *Environment*, September 1, 2005.

Pete Geddes — "Globalization: A Race to the Top," Foundation for Research on Economics and the Environment, January 19, 2005. www.free-eco.org.

Government Accounting Office — "North American Free Trade Agreement: U.S. Experience with Environment, Labor, and Investment Dispute Settlement Cases," *GAO Reports*,GAO-01-933, 2001.

Nigel Hunt — "Free Food Trade Threatens Environment, Poor," Planet Ark, April 16, 2008. www.planetark.org.

Deborah James — "Free Trade and the Environment," Global Exchange, October 28, 2007. www.globalexchange.org.

Nigel Poole — "Environmental Regulation and Food Safety: Studies of Protection and Protectionism," *European Environmental Law Review*, December 2006.

Shaban Uppal — United Nations Committee on Trade and Development (UNCTAD) *Trade and Environment Review*, July 2, 2006. www.unctad.org."The WTO and Environment," *Economic Review*, January 2005.

OPPOSING
VIEWPOINTS®
SERIES

CHAPTER 4

What Trade Policies and Practices Are Most Beneficial?

Chapter Preface

Classical trade theory was developed at a time when commerce among nations consisted entirely of agricultural commodities and manufactured items; moreover, natural barriers to communication among nations were high. Today ideas and creative works make up an increasing portion of trade relative to physical objects, and communication across continents is instantaneous. Some argue that this new situation requires adjustments to the free-trade ideal.

Modern communications that make possible instantaneous contact between people on different continents were developed long after nineteenth-century economist David Ricardo came up with his principle of comparative advantage. Those communications now enable what economists call labor arbitrage—the ability of companies to invest financial resources anywhere on the globe where labor costs are cheapest. This practice has resulted in "offshoring," sending jobs overseas that were once thought of as both high-paying and invulnerable to foreign competition. Areas where information or analysis is the primary product are prime candidates for offshoring: jobs in professions from computer programmer to radiologist have been sent overseas.

Offshoring can potentially harm workers and consumers in developed countries. Interviewed in *Computer World* magazine, Nariman Behravesh, an economist who has analyzed offshoring for the Information Technology Association of America, stated: "Some workers may have to take a job that pays less than their [current jobs]." Additionally, consumers' rights in outsourcing situations are murky. In the case of a mistake in reading an outsourced X-ray, "Is the liability going to fall on the hospital that is doing the outsourcing, the referral physician, the patient or the physician reading the image overseas?" asks Mark Bakken, who runs a company that helps to offshore radiology, in a June 2004 article in *US Healthcare*. "No one knows, and if that physician isn't U.S.-trained or U.S.-licensed, then providers really have a problem."

If offshoring is a concern in developed countries, an increasing trend toward the protection of "intellectual property" such as music, film, biotechnology, and medical advances is arousing opposition in the developing world. The value of such goods is not found primarily in the physical object, but rather in the creative ideas or scientific work that is represented by the physical object. Such goods are typically easy to reproduce. A DVD can simply be copied, specially developed crops can be reproduced by growing the plant to obtain its seeds, and medicines can be analyzed and produced at a fraction of the cost of developing the drug from scratch.

The developed world, especially the United States, has been trying to incorporate protection for American companies' intellectual property into trade agreements. The Office of the U.S. Trade Representative states that it "uses a wide range of bilateral and multilateral trade tools to promote strong intellectual property laws and effective enforcement worldwide." This policy is criticized by some for denying the benefits of new medical advances to those in developing countries who cannot otherwise afford them. Michael Lotrowska, a spokesman for the international health activist group Doctors Without Borders, noted that "in essence the United States is doing an end run around [World Trade Organization] agreements," which allowed developing countries to reproduce medicines cheaply for their citizens.

The viewpoints in the following chapter give examples of the debate surrounding offshoring and intellectual property protection, two issues among many new areas where the developed and developing world come into conflict over trade.

> "Thanks to outsourcing, U.S. firms save
> money and become more profitable,
> benefiting shareholders and increasing
> returns on investment."

Offshore Outsourcing Benefits
the U.S. Economy

Daniel W. Drezner

*Daniel W. Drezner, author of numerous books and articles on
trade policy, including* All Politics Is Global: Explaining International Regulatory Regimes, *is a professor of international
politics at Tufts University. In the following viewpoint, Drezner
argues that the labor required to produce certain goods and services cannot be used for other activities; for example, the hours a
computer programmer spends designing an interactive Web site
cannot be spent writing accounting programs. Economists call
these tradeoffs "opportunity costs." Countries benefit by concentrating on those activities that have the lowest opportunity
costs—the value foregone by doing one activity rather than another. According to Drezner, this principle of "comparative advantage" is the reason the United States benefits from outsourcing jobs. Drezner maintains that the cost savings many U.S.*

companies have reaped from outsourcing some types of jobs allow them to create new jobs and become more profitable.

As you read, consider the following questions:

1. According to the consulting firm McKinsey Global, as cited by Drezner, how much in economic benefit does the United States gain for each dollar spent on outsourcing to India?
2. What are some of the noneconomic benefits of trade and outsourcing, according to the author?
3. What is "insourcing," as defined by Drezner?

Outsourcing occurs when a firm subcontracts a business function to an outside supplier. This practice has been common within the U.S. economy for some time. (Witness the rise of large call centers in the rural Midwest.) The reduction of communication costs and the standardization of software packages have now made it possible to outsource business functions such as customer service, telemarketing, and document management. Other affected professions include medical transcription, tax preparation, and financial services. . . .

Technology Is Eliminating Jobs

There is no denying that the number of manufacturing jobs has fallen dramatically in recent years, but this has very little to do with outsourcing and almost everything to do with technological innovation. As with agriculture a century ago, productivity gains have outstripped demand, so fewer and fewer workers are needed for manufacturing. If outsourcing were in fact the chief cause of manufacturing losses, one would expect corresponding increases in manufacturing employment in developing countries. An Alliance Capital Management study of global manufacturing trends from 1995 to 2002, however, shows that this was not the case: the United States saw an 11 percent decrease in manufacturing employment over the course of those seven years; meanwhile, China saw a 15 percent decrease and Brazil a 20 percent decrease. Globally, the figure for manufacturing jobs lost was identical to the U.S. figure—11 percent. The fact that global manufacturing output increased by 30 percent in that same period confirms that technology, not trade, is the primary cause for the decrease in factory jobs. A recent analysis of employment data from U.S. multinational corporations by the U.S. Department of Commerce reached the same conclusion.

What about the service sector? Again, the data contradict the popular belief that U.S. jobs are being lost to foreign countries without anything to replace them. In the case of many low-level technology jobs, the phenomenon has been somewhat exaggerated. For example, a Datamonitor study found that global call-center operations are being outsourced at a slower rate than previously thought—only 5 percent are expected to be located offshore by 2007. Dell and Lehman Brothers recently moved some of their call centers back to the United States from India because of customer complaints. And done properly, the offshore outsourcing of call centers creates new jobs at home. Delta Airlines outsourced 1,000 call-center jobs to India in 2003, but the $25 million in savings allowed the firm to add 1,200 reservation and sales positions in the United States.

Offshore outsourcing is similarly counterbalanced by job creation in the high-end service sector. An Institute for International Economics analysis of Bureau of Labor Statistics employment data revealed that the number of jobs in service sectors where outsourcing is likely actually increased, even though total employment decreased by 1.7 percent. According to the Bureau of Labor Statistics *Occupation Outlook Handbook*, the number of IT [information technology]-related jobs is expected to grow 43 percent by 2010. The case of IBM reinforces this lesson: although critics highlight the offshore out-

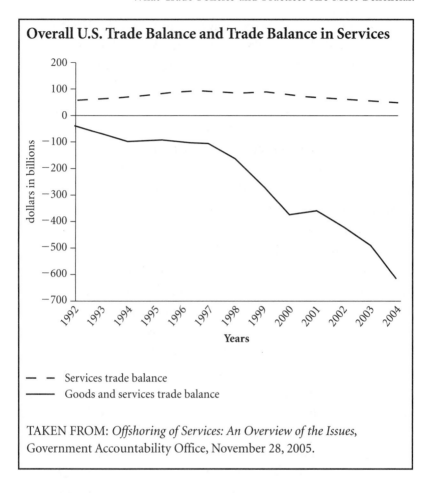

Overall U.S. Trade Balance and Trade Balance in Services

— — Services trade balance

——— Goods and services trade balance

TAKEN FROM: *Offshoring of Services: An Overview of the Issues,* Government Accountability Office, November 28, 2005.

sourcing of 3,000 IT jobs, they fail to mention the company's plans to add 4,500 positions to its U.S. payroll. Large software companies such as Microsoft and Oracle have simultaneously increased outsourcing and domestic payrolls. . . .

The Upside of Outsourcing

Offshore outsourcing is undoubtedly taking place, and it will likely increase over the next decade. However, it is not the tsunami that many claim. Its effect on the U.S. economy has been exaggerated, and its effect on the U.S. employment situation has been grossly exaggerated.

To date, the media's coverage of outsourcing has focused on its perceived costs. This leaves out more than half of the story. The benefits of offshore outsourcing should not be dismissed.

The standard case for free trade holds that countries are best off when they focus on sectors in which they have a comparative advantage—that is, sectors that have the lowest opportunity costs of production. Allowing countries to specialize accordingly increases productivity across all countries. This specialization translates into cheaper goods, and a greater variety of them, for all consumers.

The current trend of outsourcing business processes overseas is comparative advantage at work. The main driver of productivity gains over the past decade has been the spread of information technology across the economy. The commodification of simple business services allows those benefits to spread further, making growth even greater.

The data affirm this benefit. Catherine Mann of the Institute for International Economics conservatively estimates that the globalization of IT production has boosted U.S. GDP [gross domestic product] by $230 billion over the past seven years [c. 1997–2003]; the globalization of IT services should lead to a similar increase. As the price of IT services declines, sectors that have yet to exploit them to their fullest—such as construction and health care—will begin to do so, thus lowering their cost of production and improving the quality of their output. (For example, cheaper IT could one day save lives by reducing the number of "adverse drug events." Mann estimates that adding bar codes to prescription drugs and instituting an electronic medical record system could reduce the annual number of such events by more than 80,000 in the United States alone.)

McKinsey Global Institute has estimated that for every dollar spent on outsourcing to India, the United States reaps between $1.12 and $1.14 in benefits. Thanks to outsourcing,

U.S. firms save money and become more profitable, benefiting shareholders and increasing returns on investment. Foreign facilities boost demand for U.S. products, such as computers and telecommunications equipment, necessary for their outsourced function. And U.S. labor can be reallocated to more competitive, better-paying jobs; for example, although 70,000 computer programmers lost their jobs between 1999 and 2003, more than 115,000 computer software engineers found higher-paying jobs during that same period. Outsourcing thus enhances the competitiveness of the U.S. service sector (which accounts for 30 percent of the total value of U.S. exports). Contrary to the belief that the United States is importing massive amounts of services from low-wage countries, in 2002 it ran a $64.8 billion surplus in services.

Outsourcing also has considerable non-economic benefits. It is clearly in the interest of the United States to reward other countries for reducing their barriers to trade and investment. Some of the countries where U.S. firms have set up outsourcing operations—including India, Poland, and the Philippines—are vital allies in the war on terrorism. Just as the North American Free Trade Agreement (NAFTA) helped Mexico deepen its democratic transition and strengthen its rule of law, the United States gains considerably from the political reorientation spurred by economic growth and interdependence.

> *"More and more American workers will be forced to compete with poorly paid labor in the developing world, and the downward pressure on American wages could become irresistible."*

Offshore Outsourcing Hurts the Economies of Developed Countries

John Cassidy

In the following viewpoint, New Yorker *magazine economics and business reporter John Cassidy describes why the conventional theory of free trade may be outdated. The theory was developed in the late eighteenth and early nineteenth centuries, when most trade still involved agricultural products or simple manufactures. Cassidy explains that two "heretical" economists have argued that the complexity of modern manufacturing coupled with the ready availability of information can lead to trade that harms workers in developed countries overall, not just those in trade-affected industries.*

As you read, consider the following questions:

1. According to Cassidy, who developed the argument that free trade would increase overall prosperity?

2. What theory does the author say differs from the original theory of free trade?

3. What are some things Cassidy suggests the U.S. government can do to improve the nation's overall trade position?

The *Wall Street Journal*, *The Financial Times*, *Business Week*, *Fortune*, and *The Economist* have each published articles pointing out the benefits of outsourcing. Only a few journalists have dared to challenge the received wisdom, most notably CNN's Lou Dobbs, who has been conducting a virulent populist attack on businesses that shift jobs overseas. Surely Dobbs, who left CNN for a while to work at Space.com, hasn't spotted something that the luminaries of the economics profession have missed?

Classic Free Trade Theory

Surprisingly enough, he might well have. While outsourcing isn't the only reason that businesses are so reluctant to hire American workers—rising productivity and a lack of faith in the recovery are others—it is certainly playing some role, a fact that corporate executives are much more willing to admit than economists are. Moreover, economists tend to overstate the theoretical case for outsourcing, arguing that trade liberalization is always and everywhere beneficial, which simply isn't true. In today's world, where multinational corporations can produce many goods and services practically anywhere, and where investment capital can move from one continent to another at the flick of a switch, there is no economic theory which guarantees that new types of trade, such as outsourcing, automatically benefit the United States. Some Americans gain: consumers, who enjoy lower prices; stockholders, who see profits rising at companies that employ cheap foreign labor. Some Americans lose: workers whose jobs are displaced; the owners of firms whose contracts are transferred to foreign suppliers. But the economists' argument that the country as a whole inevitably benefits is questionable. . . .

It was [eighteenth-century philosopher] Adam Smith who developed the argument that the unfettered exchange of goods and services allows individuals to specialize in what they do best, thereby raising overall income and prosperity. "The taylor does not attempt to make his own shoes, but buys them of the shoemaker," Smith wrote in "The Wealth of Nations," which was published in 1776. "The shoemaker does not attempt to make his own clothes but employs a taylor." It may seem remarkable that economists still refer to the work of a Scottish radical who didn't even call himself an economist— his title at Glasgow University was professor of moral philosophy—but the division of labor, which is what Smith was talking about, lies at the heart of outsourcing and offshoring. (The two phrases once had distinct meanings, but now they are used interchangeably.)

Smith took the logic of specialization and applied it to the international market, arguing that no country should produce anything it could import more cheaply from abroad. "What is prudence in the conduct of every private family can scarcely be folly in that of a great kingdom," he wrote. This analysis implied that countries should concentrate on industries in which they are the low-cost producer, or, in the language of today's economists, industries in which they have an "absolute advantage" over foreign competitors.

A classic example involved Lancashire textile mills, which exploited the damp climate of northern England, and Portuguese vineyards, which prospered in the southern sun. In the presence of prohibitive tariffs on imports and exports, which were widespread at the time Smith was writing, England would have been forced to make its own wine (or go without), and Portugal would have had to manufacture cloth, which would have wasted valuable resources. But if free trade was introduced each country could concentrate on its strength, with

England exchanging its surplus cloth for Portugal's surplus wine, to the benefit of consumers in both places.

Comparative Advantage

The principle of absolute advantage is relatively easy to understand, and economists cite it all the time in an attempt to alleviate concerns about outsourcing. "The benefits from new forms of trade, such as in services, are no different from the benefits from traditional trade in goods," the Council of Economic Advisers said in its testimony to Congress [in 2004]. "When a good or service is produced at lower cost in another country, it makes sense to import it rather than produce it domestically. This allows the United States to devote its resources to more productive purposes."

However, some types of offshoring are not so easy to rationalize. American insurance firms are hiring workers in countries like India to process customer claims. Yet many of the Americans who are being displaced are well-educated and productive employees who could probably do the job better than their Indian counterparts. Why, then, does this sort of trade benefit the United States? David Ricardo, another ancient British economist, answered this question in "Principles of Political Economy and Taxation," which was published in 1817, and it is his defense of free trade that [former presidential economic advisor Gregory] Mankiw and his colleagues rely on to this day. Where Smith argued that nations gain by exporting goods which they can make more cheaply than other countries, Ricardo said that trade between countries makes sense even if one of the countries is the low-cost producer in every industry.

Suppose, he said, that in Portugal it takes ninety workers to make cloth and eighty workers to make wine, whereas in England cloth production requires a hundred workers and wine production requires a hundred and twenty. Then, assuming wages are the same in both countries, Portugal has an "absolute advantage" in wine and cloth. Should it still trade with England? Yes, said Ricardo. Compared with each other, he pointed out, Portugal's vineyards are still more efficient than its textile mills. Therefore, it makes sense for the country to specialize in wine production, export what it doesn't need, and import British cloth. Portugal's "comparative advantage" lies in wine. Ricardo's argument is subtle—Paul Samuelson, the great M.I.T. [Massachusetts Institute of Technology] economist, once said that comparative advantage is the most difficult economic theory to grasp—but it is also extremely powerful. It implies that the United States shouldn't try to keep hold of low-value businesses, such as insurance processing and telephone-call centers, even if its workers could operate them more efficiently than their counterparts in developing countries. Instead, it should concentrate on building up businesses like publishing and entertainment, where the displaced workers can be employed more productively. According to some estimates, the copyright business, which includes film, music, books, and software, accounts for about five per cent of the Gross Domestic Product, which means it is the biggest sector in the economy, bigger even than the auto industry. If the economists are to be believed, this is just as things should be: one industry that the United States used to dominate declines; another rises to take its place.

Economic Heresy

Any sensible discussion of trade has to acknowledge the power of comparative advantage. Capitalism has succeeded where other systems have failed in large part because it allows countries to develop according to its dictates. Poor places, like Mauritius and Indonesia, start out by producing labor-intensive goods, such as toys and clothing. Middle-income countries, such as South Korea and Taiwan, enter more advanced businesses, such as the manufacture of automobiles and consumer electronics. And developed nations, such as Japan and the United States, operate at the frontier of technology, creating industries like wireless communications and biotechnology. This hierarchy of production helps lift poor nations out of poverty. According to the World Bank, between 1981 and 2001 in East Asia the number of people living on less than a dollar a day, which is the bank's threshold for acute poverty, fell from about eight hundred million to less than three hundred million. This dramatic reduction would not have taken place if Thailand, Malaysia, and other Asian countries had been unable to export their products to the developed world.

But how does the rise of potential economic superpowers like China and India benefit the United States? Here, Ricardo's theory needs applying carefully. In a heretical but fascinating book, . . . "Global Trade and Conflicting National Interests," . . . which appeared in 2000, Ralph E. Gomory, the president of the Alfred P. Sloan Foundation, and William J. Baumol, an economist at N.Y.U. [New York University], examined what happens when a low-wage economy begins competing with a high-wage economy. Unlike many economists, who tend to rely on make-believe models, Gomory and Baumol tried to be realistic. They assumed that export industries operate most efficiently on a large scale, which means that they tend to be concentrated in one region, and that countries can learn things from each other, such as how to assemble televisions and write software. The results of this analysis were startling. "If the wage differential between two trading countries is sufficiently large, the loss of industries to the low-wage, underdeveloped country may well benefit both countries at the national level," Gomory testified to Congress earlier this year [2004]. "However, as the underdeveloped country develops and starts to look more like the developed one, the balance turns around and further loss of industries becomes harmful to the overall welfare of the more developed nation."

This conclusion directly challenges Mankiw's claim that free trade must, as a matter of economic logic, benefit the United States. It supports the commonsense notion that what helps one nation can hurt another, and that countries adversely affected by foreign competition can lose out permanently. Although the work of Gomory and Baumol hasn't received much attention from other economists, and it certainly isn't the final word on the subject, it implies, at the very least, that the potential gains and losses from outsourcing need to be weighed.

In principle, it ought to be possible for the winners from free trade—consumers and stockholders, say—to compensate the losers with monetary benefits. In practice, such transfers rarely occur. Research by the Princeton economist Henry Farber, among others, shows that workers displaced by foreign competition are usually forced to take a pay cut, that is if they are fortunate enough to find new jobs. (The average cut is thirteen per cent.) Cities hit by plant closings take years to recover, and some-such as Gary, Indiana; Flint, Michigan; and Syracuse [New York,]—never do. . . .

Disappearing White-Collar Jobs

That isn't the final analysis, however. Outsourcing service-sector jobs is a relatively new phenomenon, and it is growing fast. A widely cited example features Indian radiologists who examine X-rays from places like Miami and Chicago, and transmit their diagnoses via the Internet. It isn't hard to imagine other jobs that might be affected: reservation agents, telephone solicitors, computer programmers, accountants, database managers, financial analysts, and anybody else who performs easily replicable tasks with the aid of a computer. The jobs that are likely to remain safe are those which require physical proximity and intellectual flexibility, such as nursing, plumbing, social work, and teaching.

Free Trade Can Harm
a Developed Economy

The classical trade models, on which so much has been built, are quite resilient and adaptable to the new conditions of the world economy. The models can be modified in ways that preserve their essential simplicity, to reflect both the effect of large-scale economic activity and the rapid diffusion of technology.

However, as modified by us, the theory shows that there are in fact *inherent conflicts in international trade*. This means that it is often true that improvement in one country's productive capabilities is attainable only at the expense of another country's general welfare. An improvement in the productive capability of a trading partner that allows it to compete effectively with a home-country industry, instead of benefiting the public as a whole, may come at the expense of that home country overall. And this harm is not . . . localized damage, [like] loss of jobs in the immediately affected industry, but an adverse effect that is felt throughout the home country.

When does development abroad help and when does it harm? Put somewhat loosely, our central conclusion is that a developed country such as the United States can benefit in its global trade by assisting the substantially less developed to improve their productive capability. However, the developed country's interests also require it to compete as vigorously as it can against other nations that are in anything like a comparable stage of development to avoid being hurt by their progress.

Ralph E. Gomory and William J. Baumol,
Global Trade and Conflicting National Interests, *2000.*

One report, from Forrester Research, a technology consulting firm in Cambridge, Massachusetts, suggested that between now and 2015 about 3.3 million white-collar positions will shift abroad. Outsourcing of manufacturing jobs is also on the rise. According to Economy.com, a research firm based in West Chester, Pennsylvania, taking service industries and manufacturing together, the number of jobs moving overseas will reach six hundred thousand a year by 2010. Predictions of this nature should be regarded as educated guesswork, but they illustrate that concern about outsourcing isn't a passing fad—a situation that at least some mainstream economists are willing to acknowledge. "A huge, new swatch of our jobs will become vulnerable to foreign competition over the next few years," Berkeley's J. Bradford DeLong and Stephen S. Cohen wrote in an article that DeLong posted on his Web site. "This new set of potentially tradeable jobs are in many cases held by people who are not accustomed to layoffs. Often, they are high-paying, clean, good jobs. Some are the best jobs. The people who hold them are quite convinced that they are on top—that they have these jobs and that these jobs are well-paying—because they are the best people who deserve to have them; they are smart and industrious." . . .

At the moment, the outsourcing debate is focussed on jobs and employment security. Soon, it will revolve around wages and benefits as well. Ultimately, it is the level of demand in the economy, not trade policy, that dictates the pace of job creation. As long as the Federal Reserve and Congress utilize monetary and fiscal policies effectively to keep up spending, the economy should eventually create enough jobs of some sort to occupy most people who want to work. But what sort of pay will they command? A long-established theorem of international economics—the "factor-price equalization theorem"—states that when two countries start out with similar technology and skills but different wage rates, trade between them will reduce wages in the high-paying country and increase wages in the low-paying country until, eventually, workers in both places end up earning the same amount.

Until now, most American workers have been able to escape this pincer movement, but as countries like China and India fulfill their potential this may change. More and more American workers will be forced to compete with poorly paid labor in the developing world, and the downward pressure on American wages could become irresistible. In the nineteen-seventies, when Asian manufacturers targeted their American rivals, Japanese wages were about half of American wages, and the resultant competition was one reason that workers' earnings stagnated for a generation. Today, workers in India earn between a fifth and a tenth as much as their American counterparts. "On the one hand, economists will say that the gains from trade will thereby be that much greater for the economy as a whole," DeLong and Cohen write. "On the other hand, the potential downward pressure on loser workers in rich countries will be that much greater as well."

Some industries that compete internationally, such as pharmaceuticals and avionics, have succeeded despite paying their workers high wages, because the United States has maintained an edge in science and technology. But the ongoing transfer of knowledge and expertise to developing countries, as well as changing attitudes toward business and entrepreneurship in those societies, means American leadership can no longer be taken for granted.

Investment in Human Capital Is Critical

The essential point is that comparative advantage is no longer endowed by nature: through hard work and enlightened administration, countries can wrest it from each other's grasp. Ricardo was writing about economies dominated by agriculture and rudimentary manufacturing, where a favorable climate and the ready availability of raw materials were vital. These days, the keys to economic success are a well-educated

workforce, technical know-how, high levels of capital investment, and entrepreneurial zeal—all of which countries can acquire with the help of supportive governments, multinational
firms, and international investors. . . .

If the United States is to meet the challenge posed by a
truly global economy, it will have to insure that its scientists
are the most creative, its business leaders the most innovative,
and its workers the most highly skilled—not easy when other
nations are seeking the same goals. A truly enlightened trade
policy would involve increasing federal support for science at
all levels of the education system; creating financial incentives
for firms to pursue technological innovation; building up pre-
school and mentoring initiatives that reduce dropout rates;
expanding scholarships and visas to attract able foreign students and entrepreneurs to these shores; and encouraging the
development of the arts. In short, insuring our prosperity involves investing in our human, social, and cultural capital. But
don't expect to see that slogan on a campaign bumper sticker
anytime soon.

"The ceiling for potential damage to Western economies through white-collar job relocation is three to four times higher than it has been with manufacturing jobs."

Offshoring of White-Collar Jobs Is Shifting the Global Balance of Power

Ashutosh Sheshabalaya

In this viewpoint, consultant Ashutosh Sheshabalaya makes the case that the export of white-collar jobs is having a profound effect on the United States and Europe. The relocation of high-tech, high-skill jobs to countries such as India has a much greater economic impact than previous movements of manufacturing jobs. The end result, contends the author, will be a shift in the balance of power to India and China.

Sheshabalaya heads a firm, IndiaAdvisory, which assists corporations in doing business in India. In addition to Rising Elephant, *he has authored reports for clients such as GlaxoSmith-Kline and Johnson & Johnson.*

Ashutosh Sheshabalaya, *Rising Elephant: The Growing Clash with India over White-Collar Jobs and Its Meaning for America and the World*. Monroe, ME: Common Courage Press, 2005, pp. 7–14. Reproduced by permission.

As you read, consider the following questions:

1. According to Sheshabalaya, what sorts of workers are affected most by the latest "relocation"?

2. How might the offshoring of information technology (IT) jobs affect students' choices of career paths, in the author's opinion?

3. What other countries, besides the United States, are being affected by the growth of India's and China's technology industries, as stated by Sheshabalaya?

The relocation of white-collar technology jobs out of the West is a powerful undercurrent in today's globalizing world economy.

One study by American consulting firm Forrester Research estimates that such a process could send "3.3 million American jobs overseas by 2015." Another, by Deloitte Consulting, predicted in 2003 that Western financial companies alone would move a total of 2 million jobs "over the next five years."

These concerns mounted further when respected technology consultant The Gartner Group warned that one in 10 U.S. technology jobs might be moved out, already by the end of 2004. It followed this up with a forecast that the accelerated pace of job losses is expected to last through 2005, by when of course entire swathes of technology skills may have vanished from America. . . .

Outsource or Die

According to American IT consulting firm META Group Inc., an average of 41 percent of new development activity is now outsourced. "Going offshore and using the economics of offshore outsourcing have been the only competitive options left for larger companies since all the IT budget decreases of 2000, 2001, 2002, and even 2003," says its executive vice president Dr. Howard Rubin. Economic recovery or not, such a trend is unlikely to reverse, because there would be few reasons to.

Consultants IDC predict that the offshore component in the delivery of IT services in the U.S. may grow to as much as 23 percent by 2007, up from its 2003 level of 5 percent.

For business, offshore outsourcing is not really a choice. With time, it is likely to become even less so. Technology portal TechWeb observes:

> What about a company that needs a whole new set of applications written? They may have a few coders on staff to do things such as daily/weekly maintenance of a Web site or database, but a major project would be beyond staff capacity. The obvious thing to do is to contract the majority of the work out, and let the regular employees put in any finishing touches.
>
> After accepting bids for the job, it boils down to two feasible candidates: One contractor will bring the job home for $15,000; another will do it for $3,500.
>
> Looking at the backgrounds of the two contractors, the company finds a rough similarity in the quality of previous work done, the reliability of delivering by deadline, and everything else. The only discernible difference between the two contractors is the price—and their countries of origin. The higher price comes from a home-grown, domestic crew; the lower is from India.
>
> Put yourself in that company's place right now. Either the cash saved allows the company to do something else needed, as well as stay within budget (perhaps even to include a good chunk of a possible new hire's salary), or it actually makes the difference between doable and not.

A Real Weapon of Mass Destruction

For Western industrialized economies, their business leaders, and eventually, their political leadership, the consequences of the relocation process remain unfathomable. Intel's Chairman, Andy Grove, warns that India "could surpass the United States in software and tech-service jobs by 2010." A feature in leading American business journal *Fortune* comments that, unlike other wannabes across the world, Bangalore's claim of being a new Silicon Valley had "an eerie ring of truth." More now than a ring; a *BusinessWeek* cover story at the end of 2003 stated that Bangalore had surpassed Silicon Valley in high-tech employment; it also reported that Indians were taking the lead in "colonizing cyberspace."

The process has long moved beyond Silicon Valley to Anywhere, USA. Travelocity's shift to India, for instance, entails 250 job losses in Dickenson County, Virginia, "a serious setback for the area, which has persistent double-digit unemployment rates" [according to the *Washington Post*, February 13, 2004]. It includes not only technology giants but thousands of smaller companies too—specialized in fields ranging from chip design and wireless applications to computer animation and hi-fi codecs. Among them are typical American firms such as a business process software company called Approva, 41 of whose 67 staff are based in India.

Unlike previous waves of relocation, which involved the transfer of blue-collar manufacturing jobs, the shift now clearly concerns the higher ends of the skills spectrum—exactly where (new) employment previously (more-than) compensated for the relocation of other, lower skilled jobs. Notes *Detroit the Free Press*, "Some things never change, like big U.S. companies with high-cost labor at home seeking to buy labor-intensive parts or products from the lowest-cost third-world producer that can do the job: China, Vietnam, the Philippines, Morocco, you name it. We may not like that idea, but we've accepted it. What's new about the emerging trade brouhaha is that higher-end jobs in engineering, value-added manufacturing and information technology are migrating to China, India and elsewhere by the thousands." Unlike the past, this migration is not merely pushed by America. An across-the-board economic boom in India is pulling the process too.

Number of U.S. Jobs Moving Offshore				
Job category	2000	2005	2010	2015
Management	0	37,477	117,835	288,281
Business	10,787	61,252	161,722	348,028
Computer	27,171	108,991	276,954	472,632
Architecture	3,498	32,302	83,237	184,347
Life sciences	0	3,677	14,478	36,770
Legal	1,793	14,220	34,673	74,642
Art, design	818	5,576	13,846	29,639
Sales	4,619	29,064	97,321	226,564
Office	53,987	295,034	791,034	1,659,310
Total	102,674	587,592	1,591,101	3,320,213

TAKEN FROM: U.S. Department of Labor and Forrester Research, Inc. All numbers are rounded.

The exodus of technology jobs has made its impact felt across swathes of the U.S. economy. [As written in a 2003 *Business Wire* article,] "'When jobs disappear, industrial, retail and office buildings go dark,' says Dr. Mark Dotzour, chief economist for the Real Estate Center at Texas A&M University. . . . Not only are computer science and software design industries flourishing in Bangalore, all sorts of businesses are sending their paperwork and accounting jobs. . . to India."

Writing in October 2003, a columnist in the *Washington Times* takes a fashionable concern further: "If you want to see a real weapon of mass destruction, try a $1,000 computer in Bombay. High-tech jobs in the computer industry are bailing out of the United States. Fast."

A Grim Outlook

The grimness of this outlook is confirmed by employment trends. The American Electronics Association found U.S. high-technology industries lost 540,000 jobs in 2002 and total technology employment fell to 6 million from 6.5 million in 2001. In spite of an uptick in the economy in mid-2004, new hiring levels crucially remained at one-third of those at a similar stage in previous economic cycles. The Information Technology Association of America says U.S. hiring managers will see only 493,431 jobs created from May 2003 to May 2004, three times lower than the 1.6 million IT workers hired in the U.S. in 2000.

The downturn has hit computer programmers especially hard. According to the U.S. Bureau of Labor Statistics, unemployment among programmers has quadrupled in just two years, from 1.6 percent in 2001 to 7.1 percent in the first nine months of 2003. For technology jobs in particular, the kind of economic recovery seen in early 2004 may do very little to address the huge backlog. Worse, it may be years before the underlying composition and trend of new job creation becomes clear. . . . Fears about a de-skilling of America are both widespread and real.

Crucially, the (white-collar) service sector accounts for a much larger share of Western economies than manufacturing. In the U.S., for example, services make up 60 percent of the economy, compared to manufacturing's 14 percent. In France, services account for nearly three out of four jobs. In other words, the ceiling for potential damage to Western economies through white-collar job relocation is three to four times higher than it has been with manufacturing jobs. Such a difference will become even more obvious in the years ahead.

An Associated Press report warns: College seniors "are finding that a high-tech degree isn't the job guarantee that many thought it would be. . . . 'The entry-level positions just aren't out there now.'" Elsewhere, in Australia, a survey of information technology managers [published at CNETNews-.com] claimed outsourcing could well "sound the death knell" for the country's technology industry; the survey also found more than 90 percent of managers saying that they recommend information technology to students as a viable career path.

De-skilling in the West

Coupled to the looming build-up by India of its software and broader technological capabilities, this trend may point to the long-term de-skilling of the West—an erosion of capacities in today's leading-edge technologies, before anything realistic replaces the latter.

Demographics add another dimension to the challenge. Aside from an impending end to the West's Baby Boom population cohort . . . , these issues also relate to competition from India and China, not only from their thriving technology and new manufacturing sectors, and their growing determination to play a major role in the world, but also their far-younger populations. . . .

Consultants McKinsey, for example, forecast Indian IT exports at $50 billion by 2008, most of which will go to the U.S. and Europe. Given that average Indian wages are accepted to be a fifth of those in the West, the value of what this figure represents (and substitutes) would be five times more, or worth $250 billion. Even should there be an increase of one-third in average Indian IT wages over the period, the export equivalence would still represent about $165 billion, and at the upper rate of $75,000 per average Western IT job, equate to more than two million information technology jobs—lost, transferred or simply created elsewhere.

Other findings also attest to the growing strength of such a tide, and its often-multiplied correspondence vis-a-vis job losses in the West. A widely quoted calculation by the University of California at Berkeley, for example, shows U.S. firms shipping as many as 30,000 new service-sector jobs to India in just the month of July 2003 "while eliminating some 226,000."

Complacent arguments about the larger pool of American jobs vis-a-vis India's, therefore, miss the threat, possibly dangerously. One good example of this is *Business 2.0*, whose September 2003 issue states that the (Indian) subcontinent's "150,000 tech workers represent less than 2 percent of America's domestic IT labor force, barely enough to make a ripple in the looming job shortage." The writer, Paul Kaihla, makes serious errors at both ends of the equation. Firstly, according to researchers IDC, America's software development community reached 2.35 million in 2003. India's software development community was estimated at 813,500 in February 2004, up sharply from 650,000 at the end of 2002.

The impact of this unremitting acceleration is already recognized. According to the *New York Times*, although America has more than four times as many software developers as India, and nearly seven times as many as China, "what is more important is the fact that the recent growth rate (of software developers), and projected growth, is far higher in those well-educated, developing nations."

A Worldwide Shift in Power

Complicating the relocation debate are essentially three factors: the absence of precedents for white-collar job shifts, the continuing (and now possibly strengthening) transfer of traditional manufacturing jobs, and finally, the fact that white-collar jobs have, in reality, begun being transferred since a decade or more and already involve powerful (but rarely informed or mutually aware) interest groups.

In spite of the inherent inability to benchmark such trends against previous experience, it is amply clear that the impact of the relocation process will be momentous.

In the longer term, its implications may be staggering. For Roger Bootle, economic adviser to consultants Deloitte, the rise of India and China "will radically reshape the location of economic activity across the world." According to him, this is "the Great Displacement. It is the modern equivalent of the development of North America in the 19th century—only bigger." A more stark, endgame view was expressed by columnist Paul Craig Roberts in the *Washington Times*: As "China and India become fully employed first world economies . . . the United States might be a third world country."

Europe too is concerned, at the highest levels. After seemingly abandoning plans to overtake the U.S. economy by 2010, a strongly worded critique by the European Commission "blames low overall European productivity on a lack of investment and poor use of information technology, and warns that China and India are becoming key competitors." For French Prime Minister Jean-Pierre Raffarin, Europe faces 'deindustrialization' as a result of this challenge.

Alarm bells are ringing elsewhere too. Canada's Prime Minister Paul Martin noted at the 2004 World Economic Forum in Davos, Switzerland, that "superpowers like China and India are emerging to rival the economic might of the United States."

Such concerns go beyond economics. British daily *The Guardian* echoes Deloitte's Roger Bootle: "New superpowers (like India and China) will arise to challenge America's supremacy, just as imperial Germany and the U.S. itself were challenging Britain's by the end of the 19th century."

"Firms are more apt to invest in countries that implement strong [intellectual property] protections."

Protecting Intellectual Property Rights Encourages Trade and Investment

Daniel J. Gervais

In this viewpoint, law professor Daniel J. Gervais outlines the potential gains of stricter enforcement of intellectual property laws and notes that these laws allow inventors, musicians, authors, software producers, and others to profit from their ideas and creations. These products can be copied cheaply, and countries must enforce laws against those who reproduce books, music, software, and the like illegally, he argues. Companies will be reluctant to export legitimate copies of their wares to nations that do not protect such rights, or to invest in those countries, harming trade and economic growth in the long run, he concludes.

Daniel J. Gervais teaches intellectual property and technology law at the University of Ottawa in Ontario, Canada.

Daniel J. Gervais, "Intellectual Property, Trade and Development: The State of Play," *Fordham Law Review* vol. 74, 2005, pp. 516–522. Reproduced by permission.

As you read, consider the following questions:

1. In Gervais's view, how is foreign direct investment affected by a nation's commitment to enforcing intellectual property rights?

2. According to the author, which workers might be hurt by the enforcement of intellectual property rights?

3. How do trademarks protect the trademark owner, according to Gervais?

A simple equation cannot be drawn between an increase in trade following introduction of TRIPS [Trade-Related Aspects of Intellectual Property Rights]—compatible IP [intellectual property] protection, on the one hand, and economic development on the other, especially when measured in terms of welfare increases. There are, however, at least two indicators that are helpful to analyze the impact of increasing protection, namely (a) the increase of trade flows in goods that include a significant IP component (as compared to the physical value of the material and components—for example, a music CD or a patented pharmaceutical molecule; such areas may be referred to as "intellectual property sensitive"); and (b) the increase in FDI [foreign direct investment] concerning goods or services that require a high level of IP protection. It is essential to measure both because, to a certain extent, they cancel each other out: a company in country A (export) may have the ability to send goods to country B, but it may instead opt for local production (under license) in country B. Their analysis is based on data available from eighty-nine countries. Their main conclusion is that higher levels of IP protection are useful in areas other than fuel (and, presumably, raw resources pre-value-added transformation) and, surprisingly, high technology.

IP Protection and FDI

The traditional view, supported by case studies in countries such as postwar Japan, is that high IP protection, especially of patent rights, will lead to higher FDI. However, in a recent analysis of the FDI component and its relation to IP, Professor Keith Maskus concluded that many other factors influence FDI and technology transfer decisions, including market liberalization and deregulation, technology development policies, and competition regimes. Foreign firms invest internationally, if there are location advantages and if it is more profitable for them to produce in that country rather than licensing their IP. Firms are more apt to invest in countries that implement strong IP protections (and to bring their IP or allow for licenses in such countries). Transnational firms may also choose to invest in vertical FDI (where different plants produce products that can be used by the plant "above" it as an input to their product). . . .

Another study, this one concerning the situation of FDI in so-called "transition economies," is perhaps more illuminating because those countries were, for the most part, closed to FDI until approximately 1990. The study confirmed intuitive conclusions, in particular that FDI in IP-sensitive areas is discouraged when IP protection is weak, and that, across all sectors, low IPR [intellectual property rights] protection encourages foreign firms to focus on distribution rather than local production. . . .

In sum, economic analysis tends to demonstrate that sufficient IP protection is an essential component of increased inward FDI and trade flows in IP-sensitive goods for countries above a certain economic development threshold. The trade regime (especially tariffs and non-tariff barriers), tax, and competition laws are also potent influences.

Gains from IP Rights Enforcement

There is an important difference between increased trade flows (in this case in the form of imports) and inward FDI when economic development is taken into account. When higher IP rules allow foreign firms to begin exporting IP-sensitive goods and services to a country, local consumers and industries gain lawful access to those products and services. This may result in welfare gains. This may also, however, lead to price increases, especially when goods whose status changes to "pirate" or "counterfeit" after the introduction of IPR protection are displaced by genuine goods sold at a higher price. Increased trade flows may lead to new jobs in distributorships and the retail sector, but these are likely to be low-skilled, low-paying positions. There also may be significant gains in terms of product quality and reliability, most notably in the area of pharmaceuticals.

Inward FDI is a more powerful economic development lever than trade. It transfers technology and usually creates jobs requiring a higher skill level. This may be the case for the manufacturing of technology-intensive goods, which requires engineering and quality-control positions, as well as management and other softer skill sets. In the best-case scenario, some research and development jobs are created, which may have spillover effects in areas such as higher education, or local laboratories. . . .

As to sector-specific impacts, in the absence of sufficient rights and enforcement options, one may reasonably conclude that in the copyright arena, music, films, and books are unlikely to be distributed and national cultural industries are unlikely to develop. In these areas, the gains generated by establishing sufficient protection are "unambiguous" [according to Maskus]. However, the introduction or beginning of enforcement of copyrights may also lead to the closure of businesses that rely on copying, thus displacing (mostly unskilled) workers. Ideally, some of these workers will be able to find work in the new, creative industry jobs made possible by the adequate protection of copyrights. Such jobs are likely to pay higher wages and stimulate creativity, while reducing the need felt by local creators to live in higher protection countries as exiles. In high technology sectors, such as the manufacturing

Protecting Intellectual Property Rights

The United States is committed to promoting strong intellectual property rights through a variety of mechanisms, including the negotiation of free trade agreements (FTAs), which contain intellectual property chapters that establish strong protections for copyrights, patents, and trademarks, as well as rules for enforcement.

The United States is pleased to have worked together with many countries to strengthen IPR protection and enforcement through bilateral and multilateral FTAs. Agreements concluded in recent years include the Republic of Korea FTA (KORUS FTA), Panama Trade Promotion Agreement, Bahrain FTA, Oman FTA, Morocco FTA, the Peru Trade Promotion Agreement, the Colombia Trade Promotion Agreement, and the Central America-Dominican Republic Free Trade Agreement (CAFTA-DR) which covers Costa Rica, El Salvador, Guatemala, Honduras, Nicaragua, and the Dominican Republic. In regions such as the Middle East and Asia, the United States has used an increasing number of trade and investment framework agreement (TIFA) negotiations to enhance intellectual property protection and enforcement.

Following the conclusion of these agreements, the United States continues to work closely with our trading partners to implement FTA obligations under domestic law.

Office of the United States Trade Representative,
October 11, 2007.

of computer chips and advanced electronic components, the level of protection is less relevant due to the inability to reverse engineer and produce pirated versions and the market power of the main international players.

Trademark and Patent Protection

Trademark protection is an essential ingredient to generating higher inward FDI. The purpose of trademarks is manifold. Trademarks protect the public by indicating the source of goods and services so that purchasers can identify the desired level of quality and receive a similar product or consistent service over time. Trademarks protect the trademark owner against commercial misappropriation of the mark and/or the goodwill associated with the mark. The value of a mark stems from the mental link that is created over time in the minds of prospective buyers between particular goods or services and a particular source. Many people will buy a product or service because consciously or unconsciously they associate qualities such as value, excellence, or efficiency with the trademark. A strong trademark is invaluable because the ability of a mark to raise these associations directs a potential buyer towards a company's own product or service rather than those of a competitor. Trademarks are influenced both by sellers' perceptions about buyers' psychology and the public's marketing-influenced perceptions of how goods and services are differentiated. Trademarks also serve an informational purpose: The legal protection of marks gives companies an incentive to invest in making their marks more recognizable and easier to remember so consumers can more easily identify which particular good or service they want.

Introducing trademark protection will, as in the case of copyrights, lead to the closure of businesses producing counterfeit goods. That economic activity, however, could be replaced by jobs in distribution, retail, and franchises. These are, however, often low-level, low-skilled jobs. Trademark protection will also benefit consumers who will have access to "genuine" goods, i.e., goods that come with the perceived assurance of quality associated with the mark via domestic or international advertising and reputation. Over time, the experience in product assembly, delivery, servicing, and management acquired through franchise and distributorship arrangements may be transferred to new, local businesses.

Patents are also directly relevant. Patents do not ensure that new products will be supplied in the short term. When patent protection is unavailable, products that would otherwise infringe a patent could be made available legally for the domestic market. In terms of FDI, however, the impact is exactly the opposite, because global firms relying on patent protection need assurances about the level of protection and enforcement before considering any significant technology transfer. Fully exploiting a patent often requires expertise that is not fully disclosed in the published patent or patent application. Ongoing research and variants of the patented inventions may also exist. For this reason, firms also consider the level of protection of trade secrets for information that, for strategic or other reasons, is not disclosed in a patent. In fact, for certain process patents, even in the presence of a presumption that a product not previously available results from a new patented process, many companies prefer not to disclose new processes in patent applications. Direct patent-related inward FDI is often the best way to create high-paying, highly skilled jobs, and it is therefore highly sought after by many governments willing to go to great lengths to attract foreign firms.

Castor Oil for the Economy

From this standpoint, TRIPS was not only necessary to maximize the rent that could be extracted from emerging foreign markets, but it was also a difficult yet essential measure to jumpstart global economic development. Related beliefs hold that the misuse of "Western" IP was comparable to theft or "piracy" and that increased foreign revenues would lead to higher overall levels of research and development. IP as "policy castor oil" suggests that countries should overlook the distasteful aspects of introducing or increasing IP protection and enforcement in exchange for longer term economic health.

"The setting up of a world patent system [could] mean the end of patent
policy as a tool for national development strategies."

Tying Free Trade to Intellectual Property Rights May Hinder Development

Graham Dutfield

Many companies of the developed world started by imitating the inventions of foreigners. Today, with their economies increasingly reliant on "intellectual property"—inventions, medicines, and software—rich countries attempt to stop developing countries from copying their products. They often insist on the enforcement of intellectual property rights as a condition for opening their markets to goods from poorer countries. Graham Dutfield, senior research fellow at the Queen Mary Intellectual Property Research Institute in London, makes the case that forcing developing countries to follow developed-world standards of patent protection denies them the same path to development that the rich countries took earlier.

Graham Dutfield, "Does One Size Fit All?" *The Harvard International Review*, vol. 26, Summer 2004. Copyright © 2004 *The Harvard International Review*. Reproduced by permission.

As you read, consider the following questions:

1. What kinds of intellectual property are protected by the Trade-Related Aspects of Intellectual Property Rights (TRIPS) agreement, according to Dutfield?

2. According to the World Bank, as cited by the author, how much wealth is transferred each year from developing countries to developed countries due to the enforcement of TRIPS?

3. According to Dutfield's citing of Nagesh Kumar, how do weak patent regimes help developing countries?

Over the years, Royal Philips Electronics has been responsible for an impressive series of breakthrough inventions, such as compact audio cassettes and compact discs. What is less well known is that the company was set up in 1891 to exploit somebody else's invention—Thomas Edison and Joseph Swan's carbon filament lamp. Commercial success generated considerable revenues that enabled the firm to produce its own inventions and eventually become one of the world's most innovative corporations. How could Philips get such a good head start? From 1869 until 1912, Holland had no patent law. This meant that local entrepreneurs could copy foreign inventions for their own profit, as long as they could figure out how the inventions worked.

Ericsson, the well-known Swedish phone company, was formed in 1876, the same year Alexander Graham Bell made his first phone call. After it received some of the new devices to repair, Ericsson figured out how to make them, and by 1878 the company was selling its own phones to the Swedish public. Bell had neglected to file a patent on his invention in Sweden. The rest, as they say, is business history. . . .

Positive Impact from "Borrowings"

Setting aside the rights and wrongs of such "borrowings," the point is that such behavior, of which many more examples could be given, broke no international rules. Furthermore, the freedom to use such technologies often benefitted not only the imitator companies, but also the national economies in which they were based. Indeed, none of the benefiting countries remained copiers for long; eventually, they became some of the world's most technologically advanced manufacturers.

Might it be that the freedom to imitate was, and continues to be, an essential step toward real innovation? Evidence suggests that this was probably true in the past for Holland, Sweden, Japan, the United States, and more recently, the Asian tiger economies. If so, it might also be true for today's developing countries. In 1970, India weakened its patent system in order to achieve greater national self-reliance. This period of protection from foreign competition allowed the country's pharmaceutical sector to grow and prosper into the largest in the developing world, with a growing capacity to perform cutting-edge research.

The above question is timely because current international patent rules make it very difficult, if not impossible, for states to repeat the kinds of behavior described. Until recently, international law permitted national and regional patent systems to vary widely. Efforts on the global level by the wealthier countries to iron out these differences began in the Uruguay Round of the General Agreement on Tariffs and Trade (GATT). The result was the 1994 Agreement on Trade-related Aspects of Intellectual Property Rights (TRIPS), whose main effect was to make the intellectual property (IP) systems of developing countries more like those of developed ones.

Differences in IP Protection

TRIPS, which is administered by the World Trade Organization (WTO), sets minimum standards of availability, scope, use, and enforcement of IP rights, including not only patents but also copyright and related rights, trademarks, geographical indications, industrial designs, layout designs of integrated circuits, and protection of undisclosed information. These standards are essentially based on those of the United States and the EU [European Union] member states. Consequently, WTO members must, in accordance with Article 27 of TRIPS, make patents available "for any inventions, whether products or processes, in all fields of technology, provided that they are new, involve an inventive step and are capable of industrial application." Moreover, patents must be available and patent rights enjoyable "without discrimination as to the place of invention, the field of technology and whether products are imported or locally produced."

Nonetheless, important differences among nations remain. For example, different jurisdictions are permitted to apply the novelty, inventive step, and industrial applicability tests in various ways. They also differ in how much their laws permit non-infringing activity relating to a patented invention. Such activities commonly include non-commercial research and experimental use of another's invention. In the United States, for example, the research/experimental use exception is extremely narrow compared to many other countries' regulations. There are also variations in the range of circumstances that make unauthorized uses of a patented invention permissible for such reasons as responses to a public health emergency, and in the necessary conditions that users are required to meet to invoke such justifications. There is no single reason why these variations exist. Interest group politics are bound to be an important factor. But perhaps most importantly, these variations reflect divergent perceptions on how patent policy should promote national economic development and public policy priorities. Such perceptions are bound to vary with the divergent social and economic circumstances countries face. . . .

Moves are now afoot at the World Intellectual Property Organization (WIPO), a UN specialized agency, to go much further than TRIPS by intensifying substantive patent law harmonization in the interests of helping well-resourced compa-

Development and IP Protection

While laws protecting software exist both domestically and internationally, the concept of intellectual property rights (let alone software protection) is by no means universal. China, for example, does not enforce foreign copyrights "because it sees the development of its economy as dependent in part upon such illicit activity." South Korea also avoided enforcing intellectual property rights until it was threatened with trade sanctions by the United States. India, too, has revolted against the idea of intellectual property. When American firms considered patenting traditional Indian spices because of the disparity in intellectual property laws, many Indians complained, saying, "[e]veryone in India knows about turmeric. It belongs to us and we offer it to the world so long as they don't forget that it's Indian." In fact, the majority of the top twenty software piracy offenders are developing countries, showing there is a clear lack of interest in enforcement for software copyright or patent protection.

Mary Kopczynski, Entrepreneur.com, *Summer 2007.*

nies acquire more geographically extensive and secure protection of their inventions at minimized cost. . . .

Rich Countries' Interests

Substantive harmonization is more than just making the patent systems of countries more like each other in terms of enforcement standards and administrative procedures. It means that the actual substance of the patent standards will be exactly the same, to the extent of having identical definitions of "novelty," "inventive step," and "industrial application." Given the rich countries' interests in harmonization, it is likely to result in common (and tightly drawn) rules governing exceptions to patent rights, and the universal removal of any options to exclude types of subject matter or fields of technology from patentability on grounds of public policy or national interest.

Today, WIPO is attempting to harmonize patent law by drafting a Substantive Patent Law Treaty (SPLT) that is under deliberation by representatives of WIPO members and other participating organizations representing business and legal interests. Although such initiatives may never go much further than defining the key patentability criteria, Shozo Uemura, WIPO's deputy director-general, recently suggested as a future possibility "the establishment of basic principles regulating an ideal global patent system, according to which a patent granted in a civil procedure would have effect in different countries, and it would co-exist with existing national patent systems." For any such system to work, it would have to provide agreed standards on the scope of patentable subject matter. And it is likely, given their economic dominance, that what the United States, the European Union, and Japan agree upon, the rest of the world will have to accept.

It is somewhat ironic that Japan is probably the most ambitious proponent of substantive harmonization since only a few decades ago, the government's technology licensing policy was quite aggressive and foreign companies often felt discriminated against by the patent system and by the country's nationalistic trade and industry policy. For example, postwar Japan adopted a policy of pressuring foreign high-technology firms to make their technologies available to domestic industries. In the late 1950s, a vice minister at the Japanese Ministry of International Trade and Industry allegedly warned IBM, "We will take every measure possible to obstruct the success of your business unless you license IBM patents to Japanese firms and charge them no more than a five percent royalty." IBM had little choice but to comply.

Costs of Patent Systems

So might it be the case that by depriving developing countries of the freedom to design patent systems according to their level of industrial and technological development, we are, to use the title of a recent book by Cambridge University economist Ha-Joon Chang, "kicking away the ladder" after we in the developed world have scaled it ourselves? Or, to be even more skeptical about harmonization, would "the setting up of a world patent system . . . mean the end of patent policy as a tool for national development strategies," as Genetic Resources Action International claims?

The economic evidence yields no certain answer. In fact, it is impossible to reliably calculate the long-term economic impacts of TRIPS on developing countries and their populations. We can be certain that developing countries incur short-term costs in the form of administration, enforcement outlays, and rent transfers, and that these outweigh the initial benefits. The cost-benefit balance will vary widely from one country to another, but in many cases the costs will be extremely burdensome. According to a recent World Bank publication, TRIPS represents an annual US$20 billion-plus transfer of wealth from the technology-importing nations, many of which are developing countries, to the technology exporters, few if any of which are developing countries. M.J. Trebilcock and R. Howse suggested in *The Regulation of International Trade* that this situation indicates that "a country would have little or no interest in protecting intellectual property rights in products of which it is solely an imitator and intends to remain so—here the national interest is above all consumer welfare, that is, sourcing the product as cheaply as possible." This is the case for many poor countries. One might add that such products include not just software programs and music CDs but also life-saving medicines and educational materials.

IP and Foreign Investment

Some people might claim that the world has changed considerably and that historical experiences of the kind described at the beginning of this article provide little guidance for present-day policy makers. One way the world may have changed is that developing countries need investment and technology transfers as never before, and secure patent protection will encourage companies to share their technologies and carry out more research and development outside the countries in which they are headquartered. But what empirical evidence exists to support the notion that stronger IP rights encourage inward investment flows, research and development, and technology transfers?

Again, conclusive data is lacking, though it is likely that foreign direct investment (FDI) decisions depend on a whole host of factors including the general investment climate. A study by Keith Maskus of the University of Colorado claimed some evidence of a positive correlation, while conceding that IP rights are one of several factors that may facilitate technology transfers, and also that strengthening IP rights will involve unavoidable costs as well as benefits for developing countries. Evidence from Turkey found that the banning of pharmaceutical patents appeared to have no significant effects on levels of FDI, technology transfers, or domestic innovation. Similarly, a study on Brazil, examining the manufacturing industry as a whole, found no evidence that FDI levels were greatly affected by patent protection. On the other hand, Edwin Mansfield's influential study for the International Finance Corporation based on interviews with intellectual property executives of US corporations in several industrial sectors indicated that a large proportion of respondents from the chemical and pharmaceuticals industries claimed that their FDI decisions were affected by the levels of IP protection available.

However, research on the experience of South Korea by the late Linsu Kim, Professor of Management at Korea University, led him to find that "strong IP rights protection will hinder rather than facilitate technology transfer and indigenous learning activities in the early stage of industrialization when learning takes place through reverse engineering and duplicative imitation of mature foreign products." He also concluded that "only after countries have accumulated sufficient indigenous capabilities with extensive science and technology infrastructure to undertake creative imitation in the later stage does IP rights protection become an important element in technology transfer and industrial activities." Similarly, Nagesh Kumar, a researcher at the Research and Information System for the Non-Aligned and Other Developing Countries, a Delhi-based think tank, found that in East Asian countries such as Japan, South Korea, and Taiwan, a combination of relatively weak patent protection and the availability of other IP rights such as industrial designs and utility models encouraged technological learning. The weak patent regimes helped by allowing for local absorption of foreign innovations. Industrial designs and utility models encouraged minor adaptations and inventions by local firms. Later on, the patent systems became stronger partly because local technological capacity was sufficiently advanced to generate a significant amount of domestic innovation, and also as a result of international pressure. . . .

Denying Opportunities to Developing Countries

Despite the undeniable uncertainties, history would appear to indicate two things. First, the developed countries are being hypocritical in demanding that the rest of the world adopt their own patent and other IP standards before many of them feel they are ready. Second, and much more important, in doing so they are preventing the developing countries from adopting appropriate patent standards for their levels of development, a freedom today's rich countries made sure not to deny themselves when they were developing economies.

> *"Far from stifling indigenous culture, free trade has exposed it to new influences, and opened it to new avenues of creative exploration."*

Free Trade Promotes Cultural Diversity Worldwide

Radley Balko

Radley Balko is a libertarian author based in Virginia. He has written for publications as varied as Playboy *and the* Wall Street Journal. *In this viewpoint, Balko notes that international trade has not meant the end of local cultures. For example, the music capitals of the third world—hotspots of the burgeoning "world music" genre—are cosmopolitan cities with immigrants from many countries, places where new technology is readily adopted. In addition, trade makes economic growth possible, freeing people in the developing world from the backbreaking work of subsistence farming and giving them more time for cultural pursuits.*

As you read, consider the following questions:

1. What are some of the fears of the "Americanization" of cultures mentioned by Balko?

2. According to the author, how does McDonald's adapt its menus to differing cultures and tastes?

Radley Balko, "Globalization and Culture: Americanization or Cultural Diversity?" *www.worldconnected.org*, September 20, 2006. Reproduced by permission of the author.

3. What does the University of Buffalo study cited by
   Balko suggest that worldwide Internet use is leading to?

Anyone from a small town knows about the "Wal-Mart effect." The superstore—or a similar mega-retailer, such as
Home Depot or Lowe's—moves into a community and, within
a few years, mom-and-pop hardware stores, toy stores and
other main street retailers are put out of business. Whether
that's a good or bad thing is up for debate.

Some argue that the smaller stores go under because Wal-
Mart offers a bigger selection of goods at low prices. Consumers benefit because they can do all of their shopping at one
place, and save money in the process. Detractors say consumers get less choice, and that because stores like Wal-Mart are
national chains, they buy goods at a national level, and so local producers of goods suffer too, and soon entire communities lose their identity to mega corporations. We've become a
"Gap nation," they say.

Opponents of globalization fear that the Wal-Mart effect is
taking place on a global level, too. They cringe when a Mc-
Donalds franchise opens up in the historic heart of Prague, or
when public spaces in Latin America, China or Africa become
littered with billboards and advertisements for Coca-Cola,
Nike and Calvin Klein.

Globalization's advocates say that free trade and free markets don't dilute or pollute other cultures, they enhance them.
Trade creates wealth, they say. Wealth frees the world's poorest
people from the daily struggle for survival, and allows them to
embrace, celebrate and share the art, music, crafts and literature that might otherwise have been sacrificed to poverty.

So who's right? Is globalization killing non-western cultures, or is it augmenting and enhancing them?

Historical Fears of Americanization

The idea that American culture is encroaching on the rest of
the world is not a new one. Richard Pells writes in the

Chronicle of Higher Education that, as early as 1901, Briton William Stead published a book with the foreboding title *The Americanization of the World*. The 1904 World's Fair in St. Louis, MO, was billed as a celebration of the 100th anniversary of the Louisiana Purchase. The fair ignited overseas anti-American backlash, however, when exhibits instead tended to celebrate an alleged American cultural, political, and even ethnic supremacy.

More recently, fears that American culture might usurp the rest of the world could be traced to the Marxist social critic Herbert I. Schiller. Schiller's breakthrough book, *Communication and Cultural Domination*, was published in 1976, and was a critique of the post World War II influx and influence of American corporations across international borders.

In the mid-1980s, the debate again heated up when the dramatic [television] series *Dallas* gained enormous popularity outside the United States. The show's mass appeal seemed to validate many of Schiller's theories, and sparked "cultural preservation" movements in Europe.

But as Ph.D. candidate Christopher Hunter points out in a paper presented to the International Institute of Communications, more recent studies have shown that the worldwide appeal of *Dallas* may have been more the result of the show's ability to draw on the unique characteristics of disparate cultures than a "lowest common denominator" appeal that effectively "dumbed down" cultures the world over. Hunter writes:

> ... a number of ethnographic studies showed that foreign cultures "read" the show in vastly different ways. Ien Ang (1985) found that Dutch women interpreted the program through their own feminist agenda in opposition to the supposedly embedded message of patriarchy. Eric Michaels (1988) showed how Australian Aboriginals reinterpreted *Dallas* through their notions of kinship in a way quite contrary to the show's intended meaning. Finally, Liebes and Katz (1990) found very different cultural interpretations of

the show among Arab, Jewish, American, and Russian viewers. Further, Liebes and Katz point out that *Dallas* failed
miserably in Japan and Brazil, a seemingly unexplainable
event given the supposedly overwhelming power of U.S.
content to bowl over other cultures.

Pell's *Chronicle of Higher Education* essay makes a similar
point: that where U.S. culture has been successful in generating trans-national appeal, it's perhaps the result of America's
own diverse, immigrant population, which is able to produce
entertainment, products and services that naturally appeal to a
wide array of tastes and demand. Pell suggests that's something to be celebrated, not admonished. "In the end, American
mass culture has not transformed the world into a replica of
the United States," Pell writes. "Instead, America's dependence
on foreign cultures has made the United States a replica of the
world."

McWorld

Perhaps the most influential essay on the west's "cultural imperialism" in the last twenty years was written by Benjamin
Barber in a 1992 issue of the *Atlantic Monthly*. Entitled "Jihad
vs. McWorld," Barber's article argued that most of the third
world was either being commercialized by the West, or was
being won over by radical Islam. Neither scenario, Barber
wrote, was conducive to democracy or to development. "Mc-
World" became a catchphrase for the ubiquity of American
corporations overseas, and Barber later wrote a book by the
same name.

Conventional wisdom suggests Barber is right, and that
there is an increasing anti-McWorld backlash in the developing world. Wherever there's anti-American sentiment, it seems,
a McDonalds inevitably gets vandalized. When U.S. forces began bombing campaigns in Kosovo and Afghanistan, Mc-
Donalds franchises in those regions were the targets of protests.

But others suggest that highly publicized attacks on American corporate franchises might be anomalous. Dr. James L. Watson edited a book entitled *Golden Arches East*, which looks at how the establishment of McDonalds franchises has affected communities in Asia. Dr. Watson believes the anti-McDonalds fervor exists among just a few upper-class activists and academics, that the vitriol for American logos overseas is overstated in the media, and that most middle and lower-class communities are happy to have the added culinary option of a McDonalds or a Pizza Hut.

In most communities, in fact, the McDonalds has conformed to local culture, not the other way around. The McDonalds corporation notes that most all of its overseas franchises are locally owned, and thus make efforts to buy from local communities. McDonalds also regularly alters its regional menus to conform to local tastes. McDonalds in Egypt, for example, serve a McFelafel. Japan McDonalds serve "seaweed burgers." Indian McDonalds don't serve beef at all. And some French McDonalds serve rabbit.

Watson points out that in the countries he's studied, McDonalds has been "Asianized" more than Asia has been "supersized."

Michael Chan is the chairman of a group of Hong Kong fast food restaurants called "Café de' Coral." In an interview with Radio Netherlands, Chan said the introduction of McDonalds and its unique methods of distribution and labor management provided a template for other, indigenous restaurants in the country to flourish.

No Logos or Pro Logos?

Another important voice in the globalization vs. local culture debate is that of Naomi Klein. Klein's book *No Logo* has become the anti-globalization primer for activists all over the world. It was described by the *New York Times* as "the anti-globalization movement's Bible."

Developing World Gaining in Cultural Trade

[Here is a] troubling question: have we fallen into the dangerous illusion that the human imagination can be globalized? Many in the developing world fear that globalization, which has brought McDonald's and Microsoft to every land, has also brought Mickey Mouse and Nintendo to every mind. The answer inevitably involves considering the global mass media, whose focus, of course, reflects principally the interests of its producers. What passes for international culture is usually the culture of the economically developed world. It's *your* imagination that is being globalized. American movies and television shows, in particular, can be found on the screens of most countries. That's entertainment. . . .

As an Indian writer, I have argued that my country's recent experience with the global reach of Western consumer products demonstrates that we can drink Coca-Cola without becoming coca-colonized. India's own popular culture is also part of globalization—the products of "Bollywood" are exported to many countries, and particularly to expatriate Indian communities abroad. One Indian movie, *Kabhi Khushi Kabhi Ghum*, opened on a sufficient number of U.S. screens in 2002 to record the seventh largest weekend gross of all films opening in the United States that weekend. The trade paper *Variety* wasn't counting—but the empire can strike back.

And it's not just India. A recent study has established that local television programming has begun to overtake made-in-America shows in more and more countries; one survey found that 71% of the top 10 programs in 60 countries were locally produced in 2001, a significant increase over previous years.

Shashi Tharoor, World Policy Journal, *Summer 2004.*

Klein's book posits that logos and corporate trademarks have become a kind of international language, and that their omnipresence in the third world has robbed many peoples of the chance to develop a distinctive culture. She laments the ever-shrinking supply of "unmarked public spaces," and argues that corporations today spend far too much time branding and expend far too little resources on, for example, poor labor conditions, or on bettering the communities where they've exported their manufacturing plants.

But a recent study by a communications expert at the University of Buffalo suggests that, at least when it comes to the Internet, western cultural influence is waning, not expanding. George A. Barnett says that despite its centralization and apparent domination by the West, the Internet has given distinct "civilization clusters" a vehicle to communicate more effectively and promote their respective interests. Other communication experts have also suggested that emerging media (the Internet, and satellite television, for example) might serve as a megaphone for voices from smaller economies. The Arab-language al-Jazeera television station is one example. Most experts also predict that Chinese will surpass English as the Internet's predominant language in just a few years.

American Culture Not Dominant

There are other signs that western "cultural hegemony" might be a bit overstated, too.

For example, European anti-globalization activists have long criticized Hollywood and its big-budget studios for monopolizing the world movie industry and, consequently, polluting other cultures with American iconolatry.

But according to a worldwide 1999 BBC poll, the most famous movie star in the world isn't Ben Affleck or Julia Roberts, but Amitabh Bachchan, an Indian film star probably unfamiliar to most Americans.

Last January [2006], the *New York Times* reported that even American television programming has begun to lose its appeal overseas. *Reason* magazine writer Charles Paul Freund notes that as of 2001, more than 70% of the most popular television shows in 60 different countries were locally produced. And an article in the British newspaper *The Guardian* [in 2005] points out that the top-grossing movies for 2002 in Japan, Germany, Spain, France and India weren't U.S. imports, but were produced domestically.

The story is the same across the arts—movies, television, and literature—American pop culture exports may be well known overseas, but as emerging economies develop, consumers naturally prefer entertainment produced by artists with whom they share common experiences.

In his book *Creative Destruction*, economist Tyler Cowen also explains how music—perhaps the most accessible and identifiable sphere of a given peoples' cultural heritage—is almost always the result of cross-cultural influences.

Cowen writes that Trinidad's steel band ensembles, for example, "acquired their instruments—fifty-gallon oil drums—from the multinational oil companies." Cowen also points out that all of the Third World's musical hubs—Rio, Lagos, Cairo, etc.—"are heterogeneous and cosmopolitan cities that welcomed new ideas and new technologies from abroad."

Even reggae, perhaps the most renowned musical genre associated with a particular culture, was the result of cultural trade and influence. Cowen writes that reggae emerged when migrant Jamaican sugar workers traveled to the American south and brought back with them a jones for African-American rhythm and blues. Reggae developed over the 1950s as Jamaicans picked up radio broadcasts from New Orleans and Miami.

And yet for all of this western influence, Cowen still finds that developing countries still hunger most for music made at home. In India, domestically produced music makes up 96% of the market; in Egypt, 81%; in Brazil, 73%.

Wealth and Culture

Globalization's advocates argue that wealth invigorates culture, and that trade and access to international markets are the best way to create wealth. They point out that the Internet, for example, has given developing peoples all over the world a low-cost way of bringing crafts, textiles, and art to western consumers.

In his book *In Defense of Global Capitalism*, Swedish author Johan Norberg argues that because of emerging technology, developing countries that quickly embrace borderless trade can make the leap to western world living standards in a fraction of the time it once took. "Development which took Sweden 80 years to accomplish," Norberg writes, "has been successfully reiterated by Taiwan in 25."

As an example, Norberg cites an anecdote from the World Bank:

> Halima Khatuun is an illiterate woman in a Bangladeshi village. She sells eggs to a dealer who comes by at regular intervals. She used to be compelled to sell at the price he proposed, because she did not have access to other buyers. But once, when he came and offered 12 taka for four eggs, she kept him waiting while she used the mobile phone to find out the market price in another village. Because the price there was 14 taka, she was able to go back and get 13 from the dealer. Market information saved her from being cheated.

Norberg notes similar cases across the world, where villages in developing countries have pooled resources for mobile phone services, or Internet access, always with similar results.

The Internet in particular is fast becoming the most effective way for developing peoples to get their goods to market quickly, avoiding many of the usual overhead costs of maintaining a business. It's also a convenient way around trade barriers and tariffs. Consequently, websites promoting African, Latin American and indigenous American goods are popping up all over the Web.

Trade Creates Wealth

The wealth from access to markets, then, enables developing people to make the shift from sustenance economies to merchant economies, a transition that enables art and culture to flourish. There's little time for culture, globalization advocates point out, when you're scrambling for survival.

The late economist Peter Bauer spent most of his life studying how trade can move developing economies from poverty to prosperity. Bauer recognized in the mid-20th century that those developing countries with significant contact with western markets were also the countries showing the most economic promise and growth.

In his book *From Subsistence to Exchange*, Bauer wrote, "Contacts through traders and trade are prime agents in the spread of new ideas, modes of behavior, and methods of production. External commercial contacts often first suggest the very possibility of change, including economic improvement."

What's more, free traders point out that many times the merging of western and developing cultures often infuses new life and creativity into generations-old customs and traditions.

In addition to music, Cowen cites in his book several other examples of great artistry from indigenous peoples that, in fact, was largely inspired by cross-cultural trade. Cowen cites the famed soapstone sculptures of the Canadian Inuit, which, Cowen writes "weren't practiced on a large scale until after World War II," when the practice was introduced to them by western artist James Houston. Cowen writes:

> Analogous stories are found around the world. The metal
> knife proved a boon to many Third World sculpting and

carving traditions, including the totem poles of the Pacific Northwest and of Papua New Guinea. Acrylic and oil paints spread only with Western contact. South African Ndebele art uses beads. . . that are not indigenous to Africa, but rather were imported from Czechoslovakia in the early nineteenth century. Mirrors, coral, cotton cloth, and paper—all central materials for "traditional" African arts—came from contact with Europeans.

Cowen and like-minded globalists believe, then, that far from stifling indigenous culture, free trade has exposed it to new influences, and opened it to new avenues of creative exploration.

Technology Cultural Exchange

Opponents of globalization argue that the playing field isn't level. Free trade naturally favors larger economies, they say, and so the predominant western influence stifles the cultures and traditions of the developing world. Free traders argue that globalization enhances culture, and that, in any event, culture can't thrive in poverty. Both sides generally agree that subsidies, tariffs and other protectionist policies by developed countries against goods commonly produced in the third world (textiles, for example) hamper both culture and economic growth there.

With the onset of the Internet, satellite technology, cable television, and cellular and wireless networks, the biggest traditional barrier to global trade—distance—isn't much of a problem anymore. The Internet also makes import tariffs, another traditional barrier, more difficult to enforce.

One thing is certain: as we move forward, transnational trade will only become more frequent, and will continue to find new participants in new corners of the globe.

And activists on both sides will continue to debate whether or not the intermingling of cultures and influences that will inevitably accompany the growing global marketplace is a good or bad thing for both the developed and developing world.

> *"Products that spring from French protectionism extend the diversity of screen products potentially available to the whole world."*

Cultural Protectionism Can Create Diversity

Jacques Delacroix and Julien Bornon

Most economists believe that free trade is economically efficient, thus lowering prices for consumers. They also hold that protectionism limits consumers' options while free trade increases consumer choice, allowing consumers to vote with their dollars to buy products from around the world. In the following viewpoint, Jacques Delacroix, a business professor at Santa Clara University, and Julien Bornon, a program officer for the United Nations Educational, Scientific, and Cultural Organization (UNESCO), argue against the conventional view that protectionism reduces variety. They use the case of French "cultural protectionism" of its film industry to make their point. According to Delacroix and Bornon, the French public actually has more variety on its movie screens and television sets due to France's "cultural protectionism."

Jacques Delacroix and Julien Bornon, "Can Protectionism Ever Be Respectable?" *The Independent Review*, vol. 9, Winter 2005, pp. 353-366. Copyright © 2005. Reproduced by permission of The Independent Institute, 100 Swan Way, Oakland, CA 94021–1428 USA. www.independent.org.

As you read, consider the following questions:

1. According to the authors, how much of the United States' GDP was made up of cultural products in 1999?

2. As explained by the authors, did the French have access to more or fewer non-American and non-European films than residents of the United Kingdom and Germany?

3. In what way do Delacroix and Bornon think that cultural protectionism is affecting the diversity of French films?

The concept of a "cultural exception" to free trade seems to have arisen in large part as a result of a perceived impending American hegemony over trade in some cultural products in the 1980s and 1990s. In 1992 (unfortunately, one of the last years when the U.S. government provided such figures in convenient form), the value of U.S. exports of "communication and information" products was approximately the same as the value of its aerospace exports and more than twice the value of its electronics exports. Put another way, those exports—which exclude most royalty incomes earned abroad by U.S. economic actors—would have been enough to pay the country's considerable bill for imported clothing. Although the United States has nothing like a monopoly in this matter, this kind of export grew by approximately 10 percent per year in the 1980s and at about the same pace since then. According to [media scholar Siva] Vaidhyanathan, commerce in "cultural products" (not otherwise specified) accounted for more than 7 percent of U.S. gross domestic product [GDP] in 1999, and "copyright-sensitive" industries' exports were worth approximately $300 per U.S. citizen. In 2000, the total payroll of "information industries," admittedly a miscellaneous category, stood at approximately one-third of the annual payroll of all U.S. manufacturing. Thus, it is possible to form the impression that Americans are increasingly paying their way in the global economy by exporting such products to the rest of the world (although, contrary to a widespread notion, the total value of U.S. manufactures kept growing during the 1990s). Motion pictures and television programs, because of both their visibility and their numbers, are prominent, and increasingly so, among these cultural exports.

U.S. Cultural Dominance

Between 1970 and 1995, the U.S. share of worldwide production of motion pictures rose from less than 9 percent to approximately 45 percent. Consider all imports of movies worldwide: seventy-four countries provided the origin of their imports in the latest issue of the *UNESCO Statistical Yearbook* available to me (1999). Using only the figures given for the latest year for which they offered such figures (varying from country to country between 1991 and 1994) only four— Congo, Kenya, Tanzania, and Iran—had fewer than 30 percent of their imports originating in the United States; only sixteen had less than 50 percent U.S. imports. Notably, these twenty countries included neither communist Cuba nor culturally protectionist France. This situation still prevailed for the latter country in 2002, a banner year for the French cinema in terms of revenue.

Faced with this U.S. export success, several countries, including Canada (and within it, separately, Quebec), Spain, the People's Republic of China, Taiwan, and France have responded in a statist mode by claiming the right to erect protectionist barriers in the name of an ill-defined "cultural exception" to the generally accepted idea that trade protectionism is bad because it impedes economic development. Accordingly, the concept of cultural exception gained recognition from the General Agreement on Tariffs and Trade (GATT)—predecessor to the World Trade Organization (WTO)—meeting of 1994.

Among the growing list of such claimants, France has special interest because it has adopted the most active and most

France's Dynamic Culture

What those foreigners [from Britain, Germany, the U.S., and elsewhere] are missing is that French culture is surprisingly lively. Its movies are getting more imaginative and accessible. Just look at the *Taxi* films of Luc Besson and Gérard Krawczyk, a rollicking series of Hong Kong-style action comedies; or at such intelligent yet crowd-pleasing works as Cédric Klapisch's *L'Auberge Espagnole* and Jacques Audiard's *The Beat That My Heart Skipped*, both hits on the foreign art-house circuit. French novelists are focusing increasingly on the here and now: one of the big books of [2007's] literary rentrée, Yasmina Reza's *L'Aube le Soir ou la Nuit* (Dawn Dusk or Night) is about Sarkozy's recent electoral campaign. Another standout, Olivier Adam's *A l'Abri de Rien* (In the Shelter of Nothing), concerns immigrants at the notorious Sangatte refugee camp. France's Japan-influenced *bandes dessinées* (comic-strip) artists have made their country a leader in one of literature's hottest genres: the graphic novel. Singers like Camille, Benjamin Biolay and Vincent Delerm have revived the *chanson*. Hip-hop artists like Senegal-born MC Solaar, Cyprus-born Diam's and Abd al Malik, a son of Congolese immigrants, have taken the *verlan* of the streets and turned it into a sharper, more poetic version of American rap.

Donald Morrison, Time, *November 21, 2007.*

vocal policy of cultural protectionism (although it is seldom clearly articulated in its totality). Members of the French political elite are so serious about this matter that they have considered enshrining the cultural-exception principle in the French Constitution, presumably to prevent future governments from ever putting it into question....

Film Protectionism and Consumer Choice

We do not know exactly what would be displayed on French screens, small or large, absent protectionist policies, but we can speculate reasonably by comparing the cinema fare offered to French audiences with the offerings in countries situated similarly with respect to market size, such as the United Kingdom and Germany. In 1998 and in 1999, the percentage of movies shown in France originating in the United States was 35. (In 2002, according to recent newspaper figures, the percentage of U.S.–made movies had gone up to 52, and the percentage of French movies on the French market was only 34.) The 1998 and 1999 French figures are significantly below the corresponding U.K. figure of 53 percent U.S. movies for both years and below the corresponding figure of 57 percent U.S. movies for Germany in 1998. Yet, in absolute numbers, French audiences had for 1998 and 1999 only somewhat fewer American movies at their disposal than did their British counterparts, 159 and 179 versus 190 (both years), in spite of the obstacle of language. (French dubbing is more often than not comically inept.) In four of the six years from 1993 to 1998, more U.S. movies were offered to French audiences than to German audiences, even though the potential German market exceeds the French one. For the four recent years for which comparable data are available, the French had access to many more movies originating outside of both the United States and Europe than did either the British or the Germans, on the average: for the years 1993, 1994, 1995, and 1997, French audiences had access to 60 percent more non-American, non-European movies than did their British counterparts and nearly three times more than did German audiences. Corresponding Italian imports of non-American, non-European movies were approximately half the French figures. Thus, it would be difficult to argue that French film protectionism promotes a high degree of parochialism.

It seems instead that the advantage the French government authoritatively awards indigenous screen products has the following consequences: some French-made motion pictures and television programs that free-market forces might consign to the dustbin of visual history are allowed to coexist alongside large amounts of imported material, including especially screen material made in the United States. As a result, French audiences are presented with more or less the same fare that passes the market test in the rest of the world, with a somewhat smaller U.S. component, but augmented with French-made products and larger imports from outside their own neighborhood. Like their neighbors, the French also get to view motion pictures (and television programs) made elsewhere in the European Union. In other words, it is possible paradoxically that French audiences enjoy a more varied offering than do audiences in countries with no protectionist policy, except that they view fewer U.S.-made movies. (Remember, however, that U.S. products nevertheless are extremely common on French screens.)

Thus, if French cultural protectionists wished to argue that their policies serve both French "national identity" and global cultural diversity (irrespective of their real intent), they would not be completely on soft ground. That they seldom make such complex claims or back them up with figures suggests a built-in inattention to facts, but it does not imply that the claims have no value.

The Minestrone Argument

One might make a tenuous but not completely absurd argument that movies and television programs filmed in French (or in Spanish or in Tagalog) inherently enlarge the qualitative diversity of the world's screen offerings. According to this perspective, the commercially nonviable products that spring from French protectionism extend the diversity of screen products potentially available to the whole world, whatever the protectionist policies' real intent. The argument applies with less force to French motion pictures that could pass the market test without government backing because they tend to resemble Hollywood movies. French audiences' support of a substantial number of non-European, non-U.S. movies extends the diversity further, and this support might be related indirectly to habits induced by protectionism, perhaps because the diversity created by protectionism-induced French products leads audiences to search for even more diversity. Of course, this greater range of products is available to all viewers in the world who live in countries where the government does not effectively restrict access. That French movies and television programs are not, on the whole, commercially successful worldwide does not eliminate this argument completely: some people, somewhere outside of France, watch them or eventually will watch them. Finally, as noted earlier, the numerous French viewers contribute disproportionately to the support of the non-American, non-European screen industries even though French policies penalize the same industries (probably inadvertently).

It is not difficult to argue that greater diversity in general has intrinsic aesthetic value, that it is a good thing in itself. If such were not the case, we would expect at least some hobby gardeners to plant gardens displaying only one variety of flowers at a time. If such gardens exist, however, they are exceedingly rare. In matters of visual pleasure as elsewhere, it must be true that more is better than fewer. Likewise, minestrone soup with only two vegetables would sadden most diners' hearts. Hence, I call this train of thought the "minestrone argument."

Some of the costs associated with this (perhaps unintended) consequence of the policy are easy to delineate. An efficiency cost undoubtedly is attached, although probably only a small one borne in large part by French audiences, who have to pay more to see the same popular (foreign) products.

Some French resources are misallocated to the production of movies and television programs instead of being invested in activities at which the French excel (such as warplanes and other weaponry). The total cost to the French is probably very small in comparison to the French gross domestic product per capita of approximately $21,000 (as of 1998, according to World Bank 2000). The opportunity costs to the dominant producers worldwide, the U.S. motion-picture and television industries, are probably quite modest by their own standards, all the more so because French movies do not do very well commercially where they should, as we have seen, or just about anywhere else either. Yet France sets a bad example that might spread to other countries and to other industries, resulting in serious long-term cumulative losses. Moreover, as noted previously, French cultural protectionism may impose proportionately larger opportunity costs on the products of national screen industries almost certainly not targeted by the French government, such as middlebrow, serious Bengali or Egyptian films (and possibly Latin American television series), whose markets might be even larger in France than they already are, absent protectionist policies.

In addition, some French viewers who do not support these policies are forced to support them through their taxes. That such contrarians' objections are almost never heard in the quite-free French public discourse may reflect only the common indifference to small costs.

Finally, it is plausible, though difficult to measure, that even the small degree of freedom from competition the policy grants French producers and directors contributes to a climate in which they feel excused from having to try harder.

Periodical Bibliography

The following articles have been selected to supplement the diverse views presented in this chapter.

Bernard Avishai	"America's Invisible Export," *Civilization*, August-September 2000.
Joel Baglole	"Enter the Dragon," *Maclean's*, April 12, 2004.
Matthew Benjamin	"A World of Fakes," *U.S. News & World Report*, July 14, 2003.
Karlyn Bowman	"A Cautious Go-Ahead for Globalization," *American Enterprise*, June 2004.
Jeff Chang	"It's a Hip-Hop World," *Foreign Policy*, November-December 2007.
Carlos Marvea Correa	"Do Patents Work for Public Health?" *Bulletin of the World Health Organization*, May 2006.
Rongxing Guo	"How Culture Influences Foreign Trade: Evidence from the U.S. and China," *Journal of Socio-Economics*, vol. 33, 2004.
R. Anthony Kugler	"What Is Globalization?" *Faces*, October 2006.
Julie Milstein and Miloud Kaddar	"Managing the Effect of TRIPS on Availability of Priority Vaccines," *Bulletin of the World Health Organization*, vol. 84, no. 5, 2006.
Georgette Wang and Emilie Yueh-Yu Yeh	"Globalization and Hybridization in Cultural Products," *International Journal of Cultural Studies*, June 2005.
Murray Weidenbaum	"Globalization: Wonder Land or Waste Land?" *Society*, 2002. http://csab.wustl.edu/working papers/GlobalizationLondon123.pdf.
Oksana Zhelezniak	"Japanese Culture and Globalization," *Far Eastern Affairs*, vol. 2, 2003.

For Further Discussion

Chapter 1

1. According to Robert A. Senser's viewpoint, Americans in general support the idea of free trade. Do they believe that the United States has devised an adequate policy to put the idea into practice? Why or why not? Senser also notes that some economists, among them Paul Craig Roberts, Joseph E. Stiglitz, and Jagdish Bhagwati, are beginning to break with the consensus on United States trade policy. How do these economists' criticisms of free trade differ from one another?

2. Patrick J. Buchanan sees free trade as destroying America's industrial capability. Would Russell Roberts agree? What reasons might he give for opposing Buchanan's view?

3. Sherrod Brown is from a so-called Rust Belt state. Why might he be opposed to free trade? Would Douglas Irwin deny that free trade is hurting workers in "Rust Belt" states? What might he recommend to help these workers—something the government might do or something the workers might do to help themselves?

Chapter 2

1. What is import-substitution industrialization? Does Jagdish Bhagwati believe it works? Does the example of the Mexican bicycle tire plant in Gordon Lafer's viewpoint support or contradict Bhagwati's argument? Does Lafer give any indication that the bicycle plant is typical of a wider trend in the Mexican economy?

2. Why are farm subsidies an issue in free trade talks? Do you believe that increasing imports of agricultural prod-

ucts from the developing world will help most people in those countries? Why or why not? According to Jeremy Weber, can "fair trade" organizations help the average farmer in the developing world?

Chapter 3

1. What is the "race to the bottom"? Would B. Delworth Gardner agree that a "race to the bottom" happens in real life? If not, why not? How does trade fit into Gardner's reasoning?

2. What is the Environmental Kuznet's Curve? According to Kevin P. Gallagher, at what level of per capita national income does environmental regulation become an increasing priority for a country? Has this happened in Mexico? If so, what is the evidence that the environment is improving? If not, why has the environment not improved in Mexico, despite its increasing per capita income?

3. How might environmental regulations be used to protect industries in the developed world? Do you believe that developing-world countries should have to follow environmental standards in order to import their products to developing countries? Why or why not?

4. Multinational companies are often criticized for exploiting "sweatshop" labor. Would Robert J. Flanagan agree? At times, advocates of free trade seem to believe that trade will *automatically* produce gains in labor standards—how might Sarah Anderson and John Cavanagh respond to that position?

Chapter 4

1. What is offshoring? Does Daniel W. Drezner believe that offshoring is a leading cause of job losses in the United States' manufacturing sector? Why or why not? How might offshoring improve the jobs of American workers?

How, according to Ashutosh Sheshabalaya, will offshoring shift the global balance of power? Do you believe the examples he cites prove his case? Explain your answer.

2. Radley Balko does not believe globalization leads to homogenization. What are some examples he uses to make his case? Can you think of counterexamples? How would Jacques Delacroix and Julien Bornon answer Balko's claim with regard to the film industry in France?

Organizations to Contact

The editors have compiled the following list of organizations concerned with the issues debated in this book. The descriptions are derived from materials provided by the organizations. All have publications or information available for interested readers. The list was compiled on the date of publication of the present volume; street and online addresses may change. Be aware that many organizations take several weeks or longer to respond to inquiries, so allow as much time as possible.

The American Cause
8500 Leesburg Pike, Suite 206, Vienna, VA   22182
(703) 356-4966 • fax: (703) 255-2219
e-mail: theamericancause@gmail.com
Web site: www.theamericancause.org

Economic patriotism is a main theme of the work of the American Cause, a foundation founded by conservative columnist Patrick J. Buchanan. The foundation believes that any trade policy must include maintaining the United States' manufacturing base as a priority. The Web site contains a collection of Buchanan's columns on trade, such as "Free Trade and Funny Math," as well as columns on other issues.

Cato Institute Center for Trade Policy Studies
1000 Massachusetts Ave. NW, Washington, DC   20001-5403
(202) 842-0200 • fax:(202) 842-3490
e-mail: jcoon@cato.org
Web site: www.freetrade.org

Associated with the libertarian think tank the Cato Institute, the Center for Trade Policy Studies works to highlight what it sees as the benefits of free trade. Among these are wider consumer choice and better American-made goods due to pressure from foreign competition. The center takes a dim view of government interference of any kind concerning the economy, including restrictions on trade and immigration. The center publishes the *Free Trade Bulletin* and briefing papers such as "Race to the Bottom? The Presidential Candidates' Positions on Trade."

Competitive Enterprise Institute
1001 Connecticut Ave. NW, Suite 1250
Washington, DC   20036
(202)331-1010 • fax:(202) 331 0640
e-mail: info@cei.org
Web site: www.cei.org

The Competitive Enterprise Institute focuses on proposing policies that would make U.S. businesses more competitive in the world market. The group promotes free trade, which it sees as under attack from special interests. Policy papers such as "The Greening of Trade Policy: 'Sustainable Development' and Global Trade," and transcribed congressional testimony by its experts are available on the group's Web site.

Economic Policy Institute
1333 H St. NW, Suite 300, East Tower
Washington, DC   20005-4707
(202) 775-8810 • fax:(202) 775-0819
e-mail: research@epi.org
Web site: www.epi.org

The Economic Policy Institute states that its mission is "to inform people and empower them to seek solutions that will ensure broadly shared prosperity and opportunity." The think tank takes a moderately left-wing approach to economic issues and is particularly concerned with improving economic opportunity for working Americans. Its Web site hosts papers such as "Costly Trade with China" and "Outsourcing America's Technology and Knowledge Jobs," as well as collections of economic data.

Foundation for Economic Education (FEE)
30 S. Broadway, Irvington-on-Hudson, NY   10533

(800) 960-4333 • fax:(914) 591-8910
e-mail: books@fee.org
Web site: www.fee.org

The Foundation for Economic Education is one of the oldest organizations dedicated to spreading the message of the free market to students and citizens. The foundation works to counter what it sees as anti-free-market beliefs, including anti-trade beliefs. It publishes three periodicals, the *Freeman*, *Notes from FEE*, and *In Brief*.

**Global Development and Environment Institute
at Tufts University (GDAE)**
44 Teele Ave., Medford, MA   02155
(617) 627-3530 • fax: (617) 627-3530
e-mail: gdae@tufts.edu
Web site: www.ase.tufts.edu/gdae/

GDAE (pronounced gee-day) combines expertise in economics and technology in researching social and environmental trends in the developing world. Much of its research focuses on Latin America. Its Web site features articles such as "Free Trade Agreements in the Americas: Worth the Investment?" and "Multinationals and the Maquila Mind-set in Mexico's Silicon Valley," written by economists associated with the institute.

The Global Exchange
2017 Mission St., 2nd Floor, San Francisco, CA   94110
(415) 255-7296 • fax: (415) 255-7498
e-mail: corina@globalexchange.org
Web site: www.globalexchange.org

The Global Exchange is an organization dedicated to promoting what its members see as injustice in the international economic system. The organization is concerned with fair trade and the exploitation of sweatshop labor in developing countries. Its Web site includes information and contacts for activism, as well as a sign-up page for the group's monthly newsletter. It also hosts articles such as "Top Ten Reasons to Oppose the Free Trade Area of the Americas" and "Ten Ways to Democratize the Global Economy."

International Trade Administration
U.S. Department of Commerce
1401 Constitution Ave, NW, Rm. 3146
Washington, DC   20230
(800) 872-8723 • fax:(202) 482-3809
Web site: www.trade.gov

The mission of the U.S. government's International Trade Administration is to promote prosperity through trade and investment and to enhance American competitiveness. The agency's Web site contains links to policy documents concerning trade, including the texts of free-trade agreements and the administration's newsletter, *International Trade Update*.

**Organization for Economic Cooperation
and Development (OECD)**
2001 L St. NW, Suite 650, Washington, DC   20036-4922
(202) 785-6323 • fax: (202) 785-0350
e-mail: washington.contact@oecd.org
Web site: www.oecd.org

The Organization for Economic Cooperation and Development is an organization of governments committed to democracy and a market economy. It fosters cooperation among the richer nations in the world in channeling their assistance to poorer nations. The OECD's chief publication is the annual *OECD Factbook*, and it produces reports such as "Regional Trade Agreements Can Be Good for the Environment."

Peterson Institute for International Economics
1750 Massachusetts Ave. NW, Washington, DC   20036-1903
(202) 328-9000 • fax:(202) 659-3225
e-mail: comments@petersoninstitute.org
Web site: www.iie.com

According to its Web site, the Peterson Institute for International Economics is one of the few think tanks that is widely regarded as neutral and nonpartisan by the U.S. Congress and the press. Generally supportive of free trade, its publications also recognize the importance of American competitiveness. The institute's Web site contains a wide variety of policy briefs (including "Strengthening Trade Adjustment Assistance" and "Fear and Offshoring: The Scope and Potential Impact of Imports and Exports of Services") as well as links to books available for purchase.

United Nations Conference on Trade and Development (UNCTAD)
Palais des Nations 8-14, Av. de la Paix, Geneva 10   1211
  Switzerland
+41 22 917 5809 • fax: +41 22 917 0051
e-mail: info@unctad.org
Web site: www.unctad.org

UNCTAD assists developing countries to benefit from global trade. Areas of concern include the negotiation of equitable trade treaties and international trade's effect on the environment. The conference's Web site has numerous publications, such as the annual *World Investment Report*, which are available for download at no cost.

World Trade Organization (WTO)
Centre William Rappard, Rue de Lausanne 154
Geneva 21   CH-1211
  Switzerland
+41 22 739 50 07 • fax: +41 22 739 54 58
e-mail: enquiries@wto.org
Web site: www.wto.org

The WTO is the only international organization charged with setting the rules for global trade. The group provides a forum for countries and regions to negotiate the terms of worldwide trade. Its Web site provides a wealth of trade statistics as well as its *Annual Trade Report* and *Trade Profiles*: brief summaries of its members' trade activities.

Bibliography of Books

Volbert Alexander and Hans-Helmut Kotz
Global Divergence in Trade, Money and Policy. Northampton, MA: Elgar, 2006.

Andy Bichlbaum, Mike Bonanno, and Bob Spunkmeyer
The Yes Men: The True Story of the End of the World Trade Organization. New York: Disinformation, 2004.

Michael D. Bordo et al.
Globalization in Historical Perspective: National Bureau of Economic Research Conference Report. Chicago: University of Chicago Press, 2005.

Oli Brown
Trade, Aid and Security: An Agenda for Peace and Development. Sterling, VA: Earthscan, 2007.

Ha-Joon Chang
Bad Samaritans: The Myth of Free Trade and the Secret History of Capitalism. New York: Bloomsbury, 2008.

Robert W. Dimand
The Origins of International Economics. New York: Routledge, 2004.

Mark Engler
How to Rule the World: The Coming Battle over the Global Economy. New York: Nation Books, 2007.

Export-Import Bank of India
Trade and Environment: A Theoretical and Empirical Analysis. Mumbai, India: Quest, 2007.

Randall Frost
The Globalization of Trade. North Mankato, MN: Smart Apple, 2004.

Leonard Gomes	*The Economics and Ideology of Free Trade: A Historical Review.* Northhampton, MA: Elgar, 2003.
Ralph E. Gomory and William J. Baumol	*Global Trade and Conflicting National Interests.* Cambridge, MA: MIT Press, 2000.
David Greenaway	*Adjusting to Globalization.* Malden, MA: Blackwell, 2005.
Gene M. Grossman et al.	*Outsourcing in a Global Economy.* Cambridge, MA: National Bureau of Economic Research, 2002.
Ann E. Harrison	*Globalization and Poverty.* Chicago: University of Chicago Press, 2007.
Gary Clyde Hufbauer et al.	*U.S.-China Trade Disputes: Rising Tide, Rising Stakes.* Washington, DC: Institute for International Economics, 2006.
Kathiann M. Kowalski	*Free Trade.* Tarrytown, NY: Marshall Cavendish/Benchmark, 2006.
Pravin Krishna	*Trade Blocs: Economics and Politics.* New York: Cambridge University Press, 2005.
Tomas Larsson	*The Race to the Top: The Real Story of Globalization.* Washington, DC: Cato Institute, 2001.
Yong-Shik Lee	*Reclaiming Development in the World Trading System.* New York: Cambridge University Press, 2006.

Syed Javed Maswood — *The South in International Economic Regimes: Whose Globalization?* New York: Palgrave Macmillan, 2006.

Willem Molle — *Global Economic Institutions: Critical Writings on Global Institutions.* New York: Routledge, 2008.

Dick Morris and Eileen McGann — *Outrage: How Illegal Immigration, the United Nations, Congressional Ripoffs, Student Loan Overcharges, Tobacco Companies, Trade Protection, and Drug Companies Are Ripping Us Off—and What to Do About It.* New York: HarperCollins, 2007.

Carl Mosk — *Trade and Migration in the Modern World.* New York: Routledge, 2005.

Adil Najam — *Envisioning a Sustainable Development Agenda for Trade and Environment.* New York: Palgrave, 2007.

Laura T. Raynolds, Douglas L. Murray, and John Wilkinson — *Fair Trade: The Challenges of Transforming Globalization.* New York: Routledge, 2007.

Erik S. Reinert — *Globalization, Economic Development and Inequality: An Alternative Perspective.* Northampton, MA: Elgar, 2007.

S.M. Shafaeddin — *Trade Policy at the Crossroads: The Recent Experience of Developing Countries.* New York: Palgrave Macmillan, 2005.

George Soros   *George Soros on Globalization.* New
                            York: PublicAffairs, 2002.

Joseph E. Stiglitz   *Fair Trade for All: How Trade Can*
and Andrew   *Promote Development.* Oxford: Ox-
Charlton   ford University Press, 2007.

Alan Tonelson   *The Race to the Bottom: Why a*
                            Worldwide Worker Surplus and Un-
                            controlled Free Trade Are Sinking
                            American Living Standards. Boulder,
                            CO: Westview, 2000.

Lori Wallach and   *Whose Trade Organization? A Com-*
Patrick Woodall   *prehensive Guide to the WTO.* New
                            York: New Press, 2004.

Index